Jane Gilmore Rushing

❧JANE GILMORE RUSHING❧

A West Texas Writer and Her Work

LOU HALSELL RODENBERGER

Texas Tech University Press

This book is typeset in Bembo and Schneidler Initials. The paper used in this book meets the minimum requirements of ANSI/NISO Z39.48-1992 (R1997). ∞

Designed by David Timmons

Library of Congress Cataloging-in-Publication Data
Rodenberger, Lou Halsell.
  Jane Gilmore Rushing : a West Texas writer and her work / Lou Halsell Rodenberger.
     p. cm.
  Summary: "Study of the writing life, works, impact, and landscape of a West Texas writer. Though Rushing considered herself a regionalist, her six novels of the Texas Rolling Plains, published between 1963 and 1984, enjoyed a wide national audience"—Provided by publisher.
  Includes bibliographical references and index.
  ISBN-13: 978-0-89672-593-5 (hardcover : alk. paper)
  ISBN-10: 0-89672-593-6 (hardcover : alk. paper)   1. Rushing, Jane Gilmore. 2. Women and literature—Texas, West. 3. Texas, West—In literature. I. Title.
  PS3568.U73Z854 2006
  813'.54—dc22

                                                                            2006013560

Printed in the United States of America
06 07 08 09 10 11 12 13 14 / 9 8 7 6 5 4 3 2 1
T S

Texas Tech University Press
Box 41037
Lubbock, Texas 79409-1037 USA
800.832.4042
ttup@ttu.edu
www.ttup.ttu.edu

This book is dedicated to three good friends:
Sylvia Grider
Ken Davis
Phyllis Bridges

So, I shall try to tell the truth, but the result will be fiction. I shall not be at all surprised at this result: it is what I mean to do; it is, to my way of thinking, the way fiction is made.

Katherine Anne Porter
"My First Speech"

CONTENTS

PREFACE

My purpose in this work is to convince readers that an unbiased study of Jane Gilmore Rushing's fiction leads to the discovery of a courageous writer, whose angle of vision on West Texas's past is consistently from the point of view of women. These women were, as she has said, not just there to support their men, but to be moving forces in the region's history. To accomplish her goal to depict life realistically on the Rolling Plains of Texas from its early settlement to the present, Rushing fearlessly explores religious bigotry, racial prejudice, and the xenophobic responses of Plains communities to an outsider's intrusion. She is mindful, too, that good hearts and neighborly compassion often temper hostile attitudes in these communities on the "too-late frontier," where these settlers arrived near the end of the nineteenth century, several decades after much of Texas had been occupied.

Geographers and historians, particularly those interested in regional life, designate the topography of Texas variously. The Rolling Plains, sometimes labeled as a subregion of the Interior Lowlands, begins west of Abilene where flat cotton lands, occasionally interrupted by low hills and shallow gullies, continue westward to Snyder and the land where Rushing grew up. The land steadily rises on its western border, climbing finally up the Caprock Escarpment to the Llano Estacado plains of far West Texas. A distinctive feature of the Rolling Plains is its dual nature. East of Snyder, cotton fields dominate the almost level landscape. To the west, north, and northeast of Snyder, rough terrain, labeled the Breaks, proved ideal early in the region's history for the establishment of several large ranches. Rushing understands the divided nature of her native land when she describes the contrasting goals of settlers attracted to this region as "the difference between a man on horseback and a man with a plow"(Pyron, 11). Much of her writing reflects her response to both cultures.

Several friends, who have been as interested in Rushing's career as I, have provided information and support for this biography and critical study. Pat and Shay Bennett generously loaned me their files, which include letters, feature stories, reviews, and interviews, all invaluable to telling the complete story of Rushing's life and times. Ariel Peugh, who spent an enjoyable day with Jane and Jay Rushing as she prepared to write her graduate thesis, shared much of their conversation with me and gave me copies of her dissertation, Clyde Gilmore's "Recollections," and Jane's great-grandmother's letters. Judith Keeling shared her knowledge of the history of how *Mary Dove* was once optioned by screen writers. Kenneth Davis, who knew Jane, generously provided vital information every time I e-mailed yet another inquiry. Cherry Shults, director of Cross Plains Public Library, through interlibrary loan obtained a copy of Jane's dissertation, which gave me insight into Jane's scholarly work. Janet Neugebauer, an archivist with the Southwest Collections/Special Collections Library at Texas Tech University, provided expert guidance leading to a productive examination of Jane Rushing's papers. Early in preparation for writing this work, Jay Rushing wrote detailed letters and e-mails, which reflected his partnership with Jane in her career and his knowledge of its progression. I appreciate his kind cooperation greatly. I am also deeply appreciative of Jay and Jane's son, James Jr., who provided the photographs illustrating this work. And like Jay, my husband, Charles, has been mailer of manuscripts, copier of countless pages of text, and fixer of ailing word processors. For their encouragement, their generosity, and their enabling assistance, I sincerely appreciate and thank friends and family.

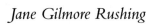

Jane Gilmore Rushing

Chapter 1

STARTING FROM PYRON

AS EARLY AS 1964, Jane Gilmore Rushing demonstrated her courage as a writer when she chose as prevalent themes in her first novel, *Walnut Grove*, the religious bigotry, racial prejudice, and anti-intellectualism so often evident in southwestern communities and small-town life. A native of Pyron, a close-knit West Texas community in Scurry County, the novelist defended without apology her belief that a regional perspective on Texas life is a legitimate approach to discovering the truth. She perceived early in her career, however, that despite her high regard for her family and their neighbors, a provincialism that often excluded the newcomer, the different, and the intellectual affected these late western frontier societies in negative ways. Subsequently in all of her fiction, Rushing, always quiet and unassuming in her personal life, relentlessly examines the chaos and pain community self-righteousness causes for individuals who have failed to conform to regional values. By the time Rushing's last work of fiction, the novella "Wayfaring Strangers," appeared in 1993, she had published seven novels exploring the tragedy hypocrisy and bigotry can foster in a society governed by inflexible rules established by religious and social arbiters who believe themselves to be righteous.

Rushing's career as a novelist was initiated with the publication of the short story "Against the Moon" in 1961. That year fellow West Texan Larry McMurtry gained critical attention for his first novel, *Horseman, Pass By*, but it was three more years before Rushing's novel

Walnut Grove was released by Doubleday, publisher of Rushing's fiction throughout her two-decade career as a novelist. Four novels set in her home region followed. Her second, *Against the Moon* (1968), chronicles both the conflicts and loyalties of a family gathered in the early 1960s to await the grandmother's death. The protagonist of her next work, *Tamzen* (1972), accompanies her father and siblings to the Rolling Plains, where she proves her mettle as a frontier homesteader. Rushing's fourth novel, *Mary Dove* (1974), takes place in the historical beginning of the settlement in the Breaks in the 1880s, where the disapproval of religious fundamentalists mars the relationship of a mulatto girl and a lonely cowboy. In *The Raincrow* (1977), Rushing presents as the protagonist a dissatisfied college professor, who returns home near the now abandoned Walnut Grove in the 1970s to mend relationships.

In 1982 Rushing left this region as setting to present her version of the controversial Anne Hutchinson's life in colonial New England in *Covenant of Grace*. Even though this well-researched historical novel attracted critics' attention, Rushing locates her last novel once again in the region she knows so well. *Winds of Blame* (1983) thematically develops Rushing's perspective on citizens' actions in a community much like Walnut Grove, where sanctimonious leaders refuse to rightfully assume their responsibility for a family tragedy that touched all of their lives in 1916. Rushing's final fictional work, "Wayfaring Strangers," takes place during the 1930s Depression years and was published in *Careless Weeds* (1993), a collection of six Texas novellas, edited by Tom Pilkington.

If read as a historical chronology, Rushing's novels re-create the century-long story of the development of this last Texas frontier. In the introduction to her hybrid memoir and local history, *Starting from Pyron*, Rushing summarizes the story of Rolling Plains settlement from her own knowledgeable perspective on the region:

> The story begins toward the end of the nineteenth century, when the first settlers came. It moves through the

years when the virgin land was being cleared for cotton; on to the building of schools and the gathering of churches; to the coming of the railroad, with hopes for a prospering town; through the long, declining years when nothing ever seemed to change; to the period following World War II when the eventual victory of technology over Pyron was no longer in doubt. The story goes even beyond what might be marked "The End." Like many other rural communities across the plains and prairies of West Texas, Pyron lives when nearly all its visible traces have vanished. That it can still be seen by the discerning eye and felt by the understanding heart is due to such intangibles as community spirit, country cussedness, and the indelible stamp of place upon the human psyche. (4)

Demonstrating that she herself possesses a discerning eye and understanding heart, Rushing acquired uncommon insight into the manners, culture, landscape, and values of her native region during her growing-up days. She determined early in her childhood that she would become a writer; and "starting from Pyron" would influence Rushing's future choice of theme, her creation of characters, and her crafting of plot. "I knew this even as a very young girl," she says. "Somehow I just felt the need to write. There was something inside of me that needed to be expressed this way" (Elder 120). As she came to know the West Texas landscape intimately, this intellectually gifted and perceptive only child listened with great interest to the stories her parents told. Later, Rushing would see these influences as creating for her "a whole unified picture of a special way of life" (Letter to the author, February 27, 1982).

Destined to have the most influence on her first works were the stories her father, Clyde Preston Gilmore, often told as she grew up. In 1994 Rushing edited and privately published a collection of her father's tales, which she began writing down about 1950 when she lived with her parents and taught at Snyder High School. She says in her note "To the Reader," prefacing the collection, that she "suddenly saw the need to set down everything I could about the way of life in those early years and to preserve some of the happenings they related from childhood." The compilation, narrated in her father's voice and arranged chronologically, was Rushing's gift to her son, Jim, and other interested relatives. In Appendix I to the privately produced volume, Rushing adds a short reminiscence her mother was persuaded to write.

Invaluable to Rushing as an informal history of her personal past, the stories in "Recollections of a West Texas Boyhood, 1897–1913" begin with Clyde Gilmore's memories of traveling in a covered wagon with his parents, John Luther Gilmore and Sarah Margaret Freeman Gilmore, from Ellis County to the western edge of Fisher County in 1897, when he was almost three. Among the first farm families to come to this Scurry County region, already named after rancher Bob Pyron, one of the earliest settlers in the region, the Gilmores soon settled in a small, unpainted, box-and-strip house. This region was distinctive because in the northeast in Fisher County lay rough terrain, where streams branching out on either side of the dividing system of low, flat hills became tributaries of the Clear Fork of the Brazos River or of the Colorado River in wet weather. Here in the Breaks, the land on this divide proved suitable only for ranching, but much of the landscape in the eastern part of Scurry County was flat prairie land attractive to the would-be cotton farmers among the early settlers. Clyde Gilmore's family first lived on the edge of the Breaks, where Clyde and his brothers helped their father farm, but they hired out as cowboys on nearby ranches during quiet times in the cotton fields.

Clyde provides details of these boyhood adventures as both farmer and cowboy in "Recollections." Rushing divides her father's stories into sixteen chapters, each recounting Clyde's perspective on some element of the developing regional culture. The traditional topics of home, school, social life, and religion are natural subjects in storytelling sessions; but Clyde also shares details of how these too-late frontiersmen and women dressed, how they shared work and play with their neighbors, and how they survived by trading. The advent of the railroad in the region, the activities of Clyde's "gang," and his experiences as a cowboy add zest to accounts of adventures worthy of Huck Finn and Tom Sawyer, as he grew up in a family of four brothers and three sisters.

Early in the narrative, Clyde remembers how his love of storytelling began. When visiting families came to stay overnight, the boys slept in one of the wagons their visitors had used for transportation. There they indulged in a favorite pastime when no one cared how late they lay awake. He says:

> Tellin' tales was one of our favorite pastimes after dark. It had to be dark because everything was too real by daylight; it would be embarrassing then to let ourselves get carried away by make-believe. We would cuddle up in a corner of the wagon, sheltered by the wagon sheet from the moon and stars, and somebody would say, "Let's play tellin' tales." (5)

Sharing his talent for telling tales with his daughter, Clyde Gilmore not only passed along his skill for crafting a good story, but he provided as his legacy a life history worthy of fictional re-creation. In her first novel, *Walnut Grove*, Rushing shaped much of this material into a thoughtful study of the boy, John Carlile, who is much like her father as a child. John's intelligence and curiosity led him as a young man to a different future from that of Clyde Gilmore, however. By the novel's conclusion, the protagonist leaves the region, likely permanently, to pursue a university education. Jane's restless father left Pyron several times in his lifetime as he sought his main chance during the Great Depression, but he always returned to the community, where he and Jane's mother, Mabel, lived the last twenty-three years of their lives.

Despite similarities in the boyhood of her novel's main character, John Carlile, and that of Clyde Gilmore, in her introduction to the 1994 edition of *Walnut Grove,* Rushing insists readers would be mistaken if they believed this first novel merely relates her father's early life. She talks of how facts become fiction "through the medium of a novel" and adds:

> It would be many years, decades even, before some of the
> people named in those pages and the true little stories
> they did actually live would be recounted in a book of
> non-fiction entitled *Starting from Pyron.* And there would
> be a world of difference between the novel *Walnut Grove*
> and the non-fiction text that could clearly be related
> to photographs of identifiable persons and places.
> (vii–viii)

Nevertheless, the tales Clyde Gilmore loved to tell gave his daughter much colorful material for her early fictional re-creation of life in her native region.

The only child of Clyde Preston Gilmore (1895–1979) and Mabel Adams (1901–1979), Jane Gilmore was born on November 15, 1925, in her Grandmother Adams's house. Her maternal grandparents had arrived in Pyron in 1904 to become the community's storekeepers. As a child Rushing rarely lived far from her native region; and as she grew up Jane spent much time with this grandmother, who with her husband, Joe, and two sons, Schley and Guy, and daughter, Mabel, operated a general store and for a time the Pyron Hotel. In "Memories of Growing Up Off the Beaten Path," which appeared in the *Dallas Times Herald* Southwest Letter series (July 25, 1992), Rushing remembers "a curious little lesson my grandmother taught me." This grandmother would frequently ask her granddaughter, "Where do we live?" Prompted to "say it all," young Janey knew to answer "Pyron,

Texas, Scurry County, On-the-Map." She continues the story, illuminating her close relationship with her grandmother:

> Then I would repeat the words, and as I remember they
> didn't sound strange to me then. It was the time when a
> child can't be sure all the expressions grown-ups teach
> him or her to say are even supposed to mean anything.
> Later when I recalled those words I thought they did
> sound rather odd, but Grandma had a lot of queer say-
> ings. Later still, I think, I solved the mystery. What she
> taught me was a kind of Chamber-of-Commerce motto,
> a matter of civic pride.

Rushing recognized early the need "to identify with a place and help
make it something to be proud of," as she says in the conclusion to the
article. Loyalty to her native region began early for the novelist,
although it would always be a loyalty tempered with her recognition
that its citizens sometimes revealed attitudes counter to her own
beliefs.

   An even more significant experience with her grandmother
occurred when Jane was not quite five years old. Grandma Adams
arranged the child's first train ride and accompanied her from Pyron
to Hermleigh, almost seven miles away. Rushing remembers the con-
ductor, the first black man she had ever seen, and his comforting
laugh when her grandmother told him the significance of the trip.
Jane recalls, "I thought he was happy because I was going to
Hermleigh on the train with my grandmother. I knew then I was
happy about it, too, and not scared anymore" (*Starting from Pyron* 8).
Later it seems likely both the coming of the train to Pyron and Jane's
memory of the comfort this man of a different color brought a scared
five-year-old would influence both character and plot in her first
novel where prejudice against blacks in Walnut Grove becomes one of
her underlying themes.

In *Starting from Pyron*, Rushing describes other events and places important to her as a child. These vivid memories of regional landscape and local past would eventually contribute to Rushing's ability to share her strong sense of place in her fiction. Among the most memorable of places was the Snake Den, no longer occupied by its namesake, where as a child she sometimes wandered alone. In preparation for writing *Starting from Pyron*, Rushing and her cousin, Billie Roche Barnard, who illustrated the work with her photographs, returned to places important to them as children and remembered them with pleasure. Rushing recalls that the Snake Den was the landmark that had always taken them "farthest away from our everyday selves"(74). She describes the effect the flat rock on a steep creek bank had on her and her kin the day they returned as they stood reading the dates and initials carved by long-ago acquaintances: "Billie and I kept standing there awhile, feeling the rock as solid as it had always been beneath our feet, seeing the familiar low hills that curved down the creek valley, one into another, to be lost at last in the misty blue distance" (80). The Snake Den as well as Paint Rock on the Pyron Ranch, where she picnicked with friends, became backdrops for significant events in her fiction.

In this history of her native land, Rushing makes an important observation revealing, perhaps more than any other of her declarations of loyalty to her birthplace, why she chose this unforgiving late frontier as the setting for most of her fiction. She remembers her two years as an expatriate in another state while her husband pursued his graduate degree:

> Once I lived for a while in East Tennessee, where the
> rains came often, the trees were giants, and the mountains
> stood up so steep and tall you could hardly see the sky.
> That is a green and beautiful country. But sometimes in
> the midst of it I would feel a great yearning for this far-

> reaching, blue-shadowed Breaks land, and the vast sky
> above it, beautiful always, in any kind of weather. (80)

In *Starting from Pyron*, Rushing also recalls neighbors and teachers, who later inspired the creation of several of her major characters. Most important, she discusses the three prevalent church organizations in the region and the precepts they impose as rules governing local actions and judgments. Significantly she provides details of the development of the "town that tried to be," which began as a dream of settlers on the "too-late frontier." In her introductory chapter, Rushing summarizes the hopeful beginnings and the declining years of her native community. With a title inspired by Walt Whitman's poem "Starting from Paumanok," which begins with a reference to his birthplace and moves on to the poet's connections with the American landscape, *Starting from Pyron* connects Rushing with her own origins and adds dimension to the facts of her personal history.

Although Jane Gilmore Rushing describes in this work her memories of living for four years of early childhood in Camp Springs, a settlement in the Breaks, she points out that she spent most of her school days in Pyron, where she graduated from high school in 1941. Just before World War II, the Pyron school was a model consolidated educational system. Students moved into a new brick school building before Jane graduated, and she remembers her teachers as accomplished and well-educated in a time when many began their careers with certification earned through examination. Never able, however, to support publication of a yearbook, the school recorded its history for the year 1938–39, when Jane was a sophomore, in an elaborate scrapbook. As an entry in a contest sponsored by the *Abilene Reporter-News,* the scrapbook won a blue ribbon as "West Texas Grand Prize Book, Division 2." Apparently the thick volume was never returned to Pyron. Fortunately for the future novelist, Jane signed on as a reporter for the *Reporter-News* in 1944, where she remembers a major accomplishment was the resurrection of the award-winning scrapbook from a dusty storage closet.

Retrieval of this scrapbook recalled for the journalist "one of the thrills of [her] high school career"(*Pyron* 66). Miss Pauline Coe, a nineteen-year-old English teacher just out of Texas Tech, called Jane in to help her unpack and catalog some fifteen new books, the first to arrive in Pyron High School "in living memory." A book lover from the day she learned to read, the student helper was encouraged to choose one of the books to take home, a privilege other students would have to wait until later to enjoy. Jane chose *Jane Eyre*, a prophetic choice for the future literary scholar, who would earn her M.A. degree in English from Texas Tech University (then Texas Technological College) in 1944 at age twenty-one.

After almost two years as reporter for the Abilene newspaper, Jane left to teach school at Ira, a rural community near her home. In 1948 she accepted a job that gave her an opportunity for two years to combine both her skills and her training when she was hired to teach English at Snyder High School near Pyron and spent her summers working as a reporter on the *Snyder Daily News*. By 1952 Rushing had enrolled once again at Texas Tech as a graduate student working toward a doctorate in English. There, more than a decade before her first fiction was published, Rushing's research led her to examine ideas that would later influence thematic development in her fiction. Her dissertation study, "House Symbolism in the Work of Five New England Romanticists," reveals both her admiration for the works of early New England writers and her understanding of the concept of art that Thoreau, Emerson, Melville, Dickinson, and Hawthorne believed they applied to the creation of their masterpieces. She was particularly interested in Hawthorne's use of symbolism and allegory to express the influence of the past on lives in the present. Hawthorne's perspective on the havoc self-righteousness can introduce into human history may have particularly influenced Rushing's own critical treatment of religious bigotry in her fiction.

While Rushing worked toward her doctorate, she was employed for the 1953–54 school term as an English teacher and sponsor of the Honor Society at Levelland High School, thirty miles west of Lubbock. After that year, she worked as a part-time instructor in the Texas Tech English Department, where she met James Arthur (Jay) Rushing, another instructor. In a 1980 interview, which Charlene (Shay) Bennett recounts in her master's thesis, Jane Rushing describes her less-than-impressive first meeting with the new English teacher:

> I was a teaching assistant at Tech and had been given an
> extra class because they didn't have quite enough teach-
> ers. They called [Jay] from SMU where he had just gotten
> his master's degree, so he came in a little bit late. I went to
> my class, and there stood the head of the department with
> the man who had come to take over the class. I had
> known he was coming so I hadn't planned to teach. Only
> *he* hadn't planned anything either, thinking he would just
> sit in class while I taught. I managed to carry on about
> twenty minutes and then dismissed the class, and we
> started getting acquainted. (39)

Despite their initially awkward first meeting, the two instructors soon found they had much in common. She and James Arthur Rushing were married on November 29, 1956. Jane received her doctorate at the end of the summer in 1957, and they moved to Knoxville, Tennessee, where Jay enrolled for two years' work toward a doctorate at the University of Tennessee, and Jane taught in the English Department. Their son, James Arthur Jr., was born there before their return to Tech in 1959. Jay Rushing continued as a professor in the English Department and later as director of the undergraduate English program, but by the early 1960s Jane had decided to concentrate on her writing career. In their 1980 conversation, Rushing describes for Shay Bennett her deliberate five-year plan for accomplishing this goal:

I had tried short stories off and on, without really any
success. When I quit teaching—which I've never really
done, but it has been sporadic—I decided that I was
going to stay home, take care of my child, keep house and
try to write. I had tried, sort of, I'd dash something off,
send it away and get a rejection slip back. Then I would
never try again. But now, I told myself, I was going to
make a definite effort to write professionally for five
years. If, at the end of that time, I couldn't claim some
success, then I would realize that I hadn't any talent and I
had better get on with something else. (45)

Rushing gave her two-year-old son, Jim, an old typewriter. He
learned his ABCs "pecking away at the old typewriter," and Rushing
began writing a novel. First, however, she had one short story she felt
worthy of publication at this time. She had submitted "Against the
Moon" once, only to receive a rejection slip, but the story continued
to interest her. Jay brought home an announcement of a short story
contest sponsored by the *Virginia Quarterly Review*. He encouraged
Rushing to enter "Against the Moon," which won second place in
the Emily Clark Balch Award contest and was published in the 1961
Quarterly summer issue. After a list of winners appeared in the *New
York Times*, Rushing received invitations from several publishers to
submit any book-length manuscript she might have. She soon finished *Walnut Grove,* a novel manuscript long in process, which Doubleday published in 1964. Publication of this novel, when Rushing
was thirty-nine, launched Rushing's career as a successful novelist, a
career that lasted less than twenty years. Nevertheless, despite her rel-
atively short period of productiveness as a fiction writer, Rushing
won the attention of literary critics and reviewers' praise for her evocation of place and her courage in choice of theme.

Chapter 2

A REGIONALIST WITHOUT APOLOGY

ONLY ONCE—in her sixth novel, *Covenant of Grace*—did Rushing depart in her fiction from her native region to create a locality with no connection to the Rolling Plains. As early as 1969, in her essay "People and Place," which appeared in *The Writer*, she explains why she is an unapologetic regionalist:

> When I began to write, I had not deliberately planned to become a regional writer; but after a while I realized that my most satisfactory stories were about West Texas, where I live. And when I wondered why, I decided it was because here is where I am familiar enough with all the elements of life that I do not have to depend upon anybody's generalizations about the country or the people. (9)

For at least three decades before Rushing began her career in the 1960s, the term *regionalism* had been a much discussed and critically debated concept among scholars. As early as the 1930s, the influential *Southwest Review* attracted essayists who attempted to articulate the definition and value of a "new regionalism." Most of them believed writers' concentration on the region they knew best might achieve universality and truth if they had a strong emotional attachment and comprehensive knowledge of their chosen area's culture. J. Frank Dobie declared sup-

port for good regional writing if writers possessed "intellectual integri-
ty," which apparently meant their treatment of regional life included
interpretation (see the introduction to *Guide to Life and Literature of the
Southwest* 7). During the 1950s and 1960s, however, the years Rushing
dared to declare herself a regionalist, most writers struggling for recognition in Eastern publishing houses and review journals avoided the
term "regionalist writer." Larry McMurtry began wearing a T-shirt
declaring himself a "Minor Regional Novelist," apparently as an ironic
and satirical recognition that writers west of the Mississippi often
earned the by-then-pejorative title "regionalist" among Eastern critics.
Although for the last two decades, a new interest and appreciation of the
"new western regionalism" is evident in academic discussions, in
Rushing's most productive years she knew declaring herself a regionalist required determined self-confidence.

In all of her discussions of the writer's craft, Rushing defends her
strong belief that her comprehensive knowledge of place enriches her
writing. In the first sentence of "People and Place," in which Rushing
formulates her theories of fiction creation, she judges her role tentatively, "I think I am what you call a regional writer." Then she
explains: "That is, for the most part I try to write stories that happen
some place in particular about people who, one way or another, are
affected by this place." Rushing dismisses some contemporary critics'
declaration that regional writing is anachronistic in a rootless society.
She acknowledges that such generalizations may originate in selected
truths, but she adds, "There is danger in accepting anybody's theory
about society, even your own, and then looking for examples to prove
it." In her opinion, a writer has to follow the classic precept of writing
what you know, even though she may not have at first thought of
becoming a regional writer.

Rushing's development as a novelist began with what she has
termed her "gathering of facts" as she grew up in Pyron, where the
railroad's coming in 1911 promised a thriving future for the settle-

ment. It was evident by 1925, the year Rushing was born, that Pyron would never realize the prosperity its citizens had hoped would materialize. Nevertheless, despite its failure to become a town, Pyron was Rushing's "starting place"; and she treasures her beginnings, which provide plot and characters for novels tracing community history. Remarkably for a native, Rushing avoids nostalgic sentimentality and examines with candid objectivity both the positive qualities of a society she knows well and its sometimes fatal adherence to a code of ethics she perceives as false. Although Rushing declares herself loyal to her native land as the inspiration for place in her work, she is never blind to the reality of living in a closed society such as existed in Pyron. Nevertheless, because of Rushing's understanding of human triumph and failure, characterization in her fiction clearly has no regional boundaries.

Writing Process

In "People and Place" and two other essays in *The Writer*, two book introductions, a conference speech, and an interview, Rushing discusses at length the art of writing as she understands the creative process in her own work. Although never collected, her perspectives on how she writes provide insight into Rushing's process of writing. "People and Place" appeared in *The Writer* magazine after Rushing published her second novel, *Against the Moon*. Commissioned by an editor who wanted to know more about the life and work of an author who so clearly believed that universal truths about human relationships could be discerned in the quiet lives of families indigenous to her native region, the essay was published as the lead article in the September 1969 issue.

Emerging from her graduate analysis of major works of the New England Romanticists and subsequently of her own fiction are several elements Rushing believes are crucial to her writing. First of all, she thinks of her classification as a regional writer as a positive judgment.

Without strong attachment to a place and knowledge of its people, writers may discover critical opinion questions the authenticity of their fictive world. In "People and Place," she says:

> You have to see landscape the way it is, and you have to
> see people; for as a regional writer you see them both
> together because you know that people are not just posed
> against a background made up of landscape, climate, and
> quaint customs. You see that what another writer might
> call "setting" is much more than that because it is never
> completely separable from the people in it. People are
> affected by place. Sometimes they are products of it and
> are content or rebellious or unaware. Sometimes they are
> hunting their place, and sometimes they have found it.
> Place is made up of landscape, climate, manners and
> morals, culture and customs; and characters are largely
> made up of their responses to all of these. (10)

Her idea of connections between people and place seems uncomplicated here, but Rushing would likely have had little patience with any critical effort to link her work with that of mere local color fiction, which depended on superficial description of customs, folklore, dialect, and dress to create place.

A confident sense of place comes first in her creative process, but Rushing understands the power of the unexpected directions a writer's imagination may lead in artistic creation. In "The Roots of a Novel," which examines the evolution of her novel *Mary Dove*, Rushing says all of her fiction "seems to have sprouted out of her West Texas background like mesquite out of a prairie pasture." She explains her metaphor:

> I think of mesquite because it is stubborn, deep rooted,
> hard to eradicate from land where farmers and ranchers

want other plants to grow. My intimate relationship to
the country I was born and raised in, and still go back to
when I can, seems that tenacious. I have some ideas for
books . . . that don't have a thing to do with the wide
skies, the sweeping horizons, the rocky creeks and hills of
West Texas; but whenever I think I am on the point of
cultivating a new strain, the old roots stir and the native
growth asserts itself. (9)

The author admits that in her search for the verities in West Texas
life she has come to realize that experience and knowledge of the
region's history are not enough. A deeper examination of regional
values and their effect on human life requires a sometimes inexplica-
ble passion. For Rushing, the process of writing *Mary Dove* provided
her, if not with a poetic epiphany, certainly some insight into her creative imagination when the search for truth in the imagined life of an
isolated young woman on the West Texas frontier became "a deep and
abiding concern"("Roots" 10). For this novel, inspiration invaded
Rushing's imagination uninvited and blossomed into an unexpected
plot and intriguing characters suggesting a story demanding to be
told. She admits in "The Roots of a Novel" that she has no clue as to
how a writer's imagination functions, but for *Mary Dove* she found
that so powerful was her need to record the tale emerging in her consciousness that she "barely spoke to anyone" until she discovered who
her characters would be. It all began with her visit to the ranch country in the Breaks to find material she needed for an article she was
writing. Then, she says, "Something took hold of me there, something
I couldn't get free of even after the article was finished"(9). She wrote
Mary Dove in record time, out of compulsion, she says in retrospect.

Rushing refuses to classify *Mary Dove* as historical fiction. Set in
the Breaks during the formative years of the "too-late frontier," she
thinks of this novel as well as of all her Walnut Grove novels as "period
pieces." After she published her fifth novel, *The Raincrow*, however, she

was finally ready to tackle what she defined as historical fiction. In "Setting in the Historical Novel," published in *The Writer* in 1984, Rushing reflects on the special demands of writing fiction based on historical events. In her discussion of her sixth novel, *Covenant of Grace,* she warns that once a writer chooses to re-create a historical figure or event in fiction, only intense research produces the material that in turn can be shaped into a realistic, believable novel. Her research into the near-mythical tragic life of the charismatic Anne Hutchinson in colonial New England began with her longtime interest and scholarly study of the colonial writer Anne Bradstreet's life and poetry. Rushing admits that even after years of research "you can never really know everything about any period," but for this book, she immersed herself in the "intellectual atmosphere" of the earliest settlements in America. By the end of each day, she says it was difficult to "wrench [herself] away from . . . seventeenth-century Boston" ("Setting" 13).

In this essay, the author methodically examines research techniques as a component of her creative work. However, she shares little information on her methods for characterization. Later, after she published her last novel, *Winds of Blame,* Rushing discovered in retrospect that without conscious intent, she has portrayed a person she perceives as a dominant figure in most of her works. At least one determined woman with great strength of personality and the grit necessary to prevail in the demanding landscape of Rushing's settings appears in each of her novels. Such a character, she says in her essay, "The Grandmother of West Texas" in *Texas Women: The Myth, the Reality,* reflects attitudes that sturdy West Texas women have held since settlement days in this unpredictable land. She had certainly not intended, she says, to make grandmothers a leitmotif in her work. Nevertheless, this grandmother figure or young grandmother-in-the-making, representative of the "fundamentalist-traditionalist values" that influenced family and community life, appears regularly in her fiction, often as the protagonist.

Grandmother Adams's stories of her youth, as well as the author's later mature consideration of this maternal grandmother's role and influence on her family, provided the novelist with ample material for the creation of the Grandmother of West Texas. Rushing describes Lora Adams as full of fun with a strong romantic streak, but "overshadowing these light-hearted traits," the author says, "was her iron-bound Puritan morality, which formed the firm foundation of her being" ("The Grandmother" 39). Determination to stay the course, no matter what hardships early life on the frontier presented, this strong-minded woman was tenacious in her loyalty to her family and compassionate in her concern for the welfare of her community. Sometimes this regard for her neighbors' well-being also led, through assessment of the "looks of the thing," to both stern judgment and what in turn might be classified as gossip. The tension between the good works of such women in Rushing's novels and their sometimes busybody criticism of other's actions often leads to conflict and, in some cases, to tragic consequences in her fiction. In her essays discussing her work and techniques, Rushing leaves few questions about her creative process unanswered.

Even though Rushing's fiction has been inspired by her comprehensive knowledge of regional life and lore, she found each novel, except perhaps for *Mary Dove*, required a gestation period during which she thought through a project thoroughly before she began writing. She described her working day in an interview with Shay Bennett:

> During the school term, I work about three hours in the morning and three in the afternoon. Of course, I'm not always steadily working, but I try to have the time available. I have always typed everything. This book I'm working on [*Covenant of Grace*], however, seems to be more comfortable to write in longhand. Before the day is over, though, I type what I've written. I depend on my hus-

band quite a bit for early revision. He always reads the
first draft that I can bear to show anyone and frequently
has good suggestions. (55)

Usually, a novel manuscript requires at least a year to complete, she
adds.

She published her last novel, *Winds of Blame,* in 1982; and retro-
spectively in her introduction to a 1992 reprint of *Walnut Grove,* she
sums up in a few paragraphs all she has learned about her craft in the
twenty years in which she published seven novels. She says shaping
"still describes . . . as well as any one word could the writing of fiction." Rushing compares the writer to a sculptor, who "finds in a
block of stone the shape that speaks to him." She adds, "[T]he novelist tries to carve out of a mass of true tales, impressions, memories, and
carefully gathered facts a book that will reveal and illumine a time, a
place, or a way of life and thought that has in some way moved her."

Rushing concludes these observations on the writing process by
pointing out that the "shaping of plot and characters, the choice of
descriptive details, the portrayal of inward hopes, perplexities, or
philosophies, are determined by the author's perception of the novel's
essential qualities" (*Walnut Grove* viii). Those essential qualities originate for Rushing in a thorough knowledge of place and people, a
receptive and vivid imagination, and a willingness to pursue truth
through intensive research.

Influences

FOLK CULTURE

Even though Rushing's lifelong unflinching and honest observation
of her native region has provided a catalog of a society's failings, she
nevertheless appreciated the community's positive contributions to
her career as a writer. Rushing and her husband were collectors of
folklore, particularly of the games they played and stories they heard
as children. In 1997 the Christmas booklet with a bright red cover she

and Jay assembled to send to friends, included a series of nonsensical verses children once liked to recite; several games children played during her childhood; and a "jump story," one of the scary tales Jay's grandfather liked to tell his grandchildren. Inclusion of this remembered lore from her past adds zest and realism to her novels. Rushing found other sources as well for re-creating the lives of early West Texans. In her interview with Iva Elder, Rushing describes her conversation at a conference with the historian J. Evetts Haley, who invited her to look through his private files of old-timers' stories (Elder 124). Rushing welcomed such primary material, but she most valued her knowledge of oral history, folk sayings, superstitions, ballads, and games associated with Rolling Plains frontier life. Authenticity in her re-creation of this region's folk culture depended upon the understanding she acquired from stories she heard and experiences she remembered. Her family's tales, designated as family saga by folklorists, influence characterization, narrative action, and theme in all of Rushing's West Texas novels.

In *Walnut Grove*, Rushing describes the activities of an early pioneer boy, based on her father's stories. Boys of his generation needed to know how to whittle wood, trade wisely for friends' coveted possessions, play mumble peg with knives, and shoot marbles. They carried their sausage and biscuit lunches in syrup buckets to a one-room school, where they brought their drinking water in buckets from a windmill half a mile away. They grew up attending play-parties where "swinging games" substituted for the dances church leaders forbade. Dancing to fiddle music was considered a sin; playing games was not. Singers, rather than square dance callers, inspired by band accompaniment, indicated the movements as party goers swung to "Skip to My Lou," "Miller Boy," "Shoot the Buffalo," and "Sandy Land." Often such parties were publicized as ice cream suppers, and the entire community attended. Much of this lore, as well as the vernacular of early settlers, Rushing learned from her parents' and grandparents' accounts of early experiences in West Texas.

In both her prize-winning short story, "Against the Moon," her first major publication, and her second novel with the same title, Rushing's character portrayal is based largely on family stories and her childhood memories. The novel expands a rural family's gathering to await a matriarch's death into a fully developed narrative, but even in the short story she recaptures relatives' activities after their arrival and before the death of her great-grandmother Freeman, who lay comatose in the summer of 1935. In her introduction to the 1991 reprint of her novel *Against the Moon*, the author describes nine-year-old Jane's memory of cousins "drifting around the place in little bunches." She recalls that "[t]he mysterious feelings in the air around us may have made us do strange things" (vi). Most vividly, she recalls her grandfather's declaration that thunderstorms won't come up against the moon. Recollection of this folk belief that no drouth ever broke as the moon wanes initiates Rushing's creation of both plot and character in these works. She describes this memory:

> I remembered a night when a thunderstorm seemed to
> be brewing. There was a bright moon shining, but dark
> clouds piled up in the western sky and lightning flashed
> far off. I can see it now. Men and women stand out in the
> yard looking anxiously at the sky, talking a lot, worrying
> and prophesying. Somehow above it all I hear my grand-
> father's voice. I don't see him, I don't know where he is,
> whether in or out of the house; but he is there some-
> where, in all his strength and wisdom. "A cloud won't
> come up against the moon," he says. (vii)

Folk belief provided the title for yet another of Rushing's novels. For her fifth novel set on the Rolling Plains, Rushing chose the near-mythical West Texas rain prophet, the raincrow, as inspiration for her title and as a symbol providing the underlying framework for this work. The narrator of *The Raincrow*, Gail Messenger, recalls that even from childhood she has tried to interpret the elusive bird's cry, believing secretly and illogically, as she does throughout her long summer's visit home for the first time in many years, that somehow learning the raincrow's secret message will bring the solution to her own personal problems. In the end, the discovery that the raincrow's prophecy is frequently false and that furthermore the bird belongs to the cuckoo family illustrates Rushing's ability to provide an ironic twist to the traditional beliefs she grew up hearing.

In all of her Walnut Grove novels, Rushing also depends upon her knowledge of ballads, beliefs, sayings, and customs to convey an authentic sense of place and to add dimension to characterization. For example, Rushing captures the feeling of goodwill citizens demonstrated when they came together for picnics and church activities in her descriptions of these gatherings. One of the annual social gatherings in *Winds of Blame* occurs when the men of the community gather for the traditional drive of crop-eating rabbits into a corral where they are destroyed. Afterward, the men and their families enjoy a barbecue picnic meal to celebrate their success. In *Walnut Grove*, details of the town site opening include a description of the rituals of cooking massive amounts of barbecue, socializing with neighbors gathered in town to celebrate, and listening to politician's speeches, all typical of early observances of the arrival of the train for the first time in a West Texas settlement.

Rushing includes titles and often words to party songs and ballads the settlers sang. Because he knows his mulatto daughter will never be accepted by the white settlers as an equal, the sheepman Pardue eases the loneliness of his isolated young daughter in *Mary Dove* by teaching her to strum the guitar and sing traditional ballads, including "Listen to the Mocking Bird," "Barb'ry Ellen," and "Mohee." Rushing records the words of "Mohee" as part of Mary Dove's questioning whether her cowboy lover will return to her and "spend the rest of [his] days with little Mohee" (176). Establishing sense of place for Rushing depends largely on her familiarity with West Texas lore and her ability to connect her characters with their regional culture through their customs and social activities associated with church, school, and parties.

Rushing's realistic portrayal of frontier and rural women emanates from her knowledge of how her grandmothers and their peers coped with West Texas weather and hardships. A country woman's habit becomes solace for Lizzie Doane, the abused and ailing wife in *Winds of Blame*, as she seeks comfort from her troubles. Rushing describes how Lizzie chews a hackberry twig into a brush, dips it into her snuff jar, and with a satisfied sigh, places it into her mouth. In her story of the young pioneer woman Tamzen, Rushing emphasizes her protagonist's self-sufficiency when she provides details of how Tamzen stretches sewn-together flour sacks above her living room as a ceiling to protect the family from sifting West Texas sand. She carpets her floor with burlap "tow sacks" made colorful by boiling them in a wash pot with an old, red flannel nightgown. The author values vivid images such as these remembered from her grandmothers' tales and the customs she observed as a child in Pyron. In most cases, they provide the seeds from which her fiction springs.

NATURE AND LANDSCAPE

Family stories and regional folklore provide skeletal framework and realistic detail in Rushing's works, but she also grew up especially aware of the natural world around her. Evidence of Rushing's close association of Rolling Plains life with its natural surroundings emerges in all of her fiction. The writer's love of the Rolling Plains landscape and natural phenomena is reflected in her colorful descriptions of sunsets, of the terrain of both the prairie and the Breaks, and of quiet places where her protagonists go for escape from troubling problems.

In the author's fourth novel, Mary Dove identifies so closely with the mourning dove by her bathing pool that she sometimes wonders if she is named after the dove or the dove after her. John Carlile, distressed that his Walnut Grove friends have no time to go camping, heads for Mulberry Hollow, where a spring-fed pool provides a good fishing hole and where he once dreamed of becoming Lone Eagle, who "would defend to the death whatever was right" (*Walnut Grove* 161). On a drive with her friend Archie, Isabel Doane, in *Winds of Blame,* admits as they stand looking out "across the rugged brown prairie, marked with a line of green where the creek cut through the Doane land," that, although she lives on farmland, she loves the Breaks best, where a pool with the hackberry trees shading it serves as a good picnic spot for the two (212).

In a letter *The Writer* published alongside her essay "People and Place," Rushing remembers how this land of rocks, hills, and prairie inspired her own ambition to become a writer:

> This is a wonderful, lonely, understated sort of country. As a child planning to become a writer, I used to go off in the pasture as far as I could and try to fit myself into situations to match the literary-sounding descriptions I liked. "As far as the eye could see, there was no sign of human habitation." (It was awfully hard to get located so as not to see at least a windmill sticking up somewhere.) Or "Not a sound could be heard except singing of the July flies in the mesquite trees." I haven't half said how that country really is; I hope I can some day; I intend to keep trying (11).

Rushing wrote this letter in 1969 after she had already initiated the cycle she predicts with publication of *Walnut Grove* (1964) and *Against the Moon* (1968).

Later in *The Raincrow,* protagonist Gail Messenger, with whom the writer said she identified, echoes Rushing's kinship with her native landscape. Gail deliberately sets out one summer morning for her place of childhood daydreaming:

Cow trails that lead me forth on my pasture walk slope
gently down through summer-brown grass and scattered
mesquite to the head of a shallow draw where the grass
(in a rainy season) stays green all summer long. On any
day after school I might come this far. On many a summer morning I was led here, to dream beneath the
twisted branches of an uncommonly ancient mesquite
tree, as I gazed at the sky through the delicate tracery of
its slender leaves. (31)

Even though Rushing obviously loved the Rolling Plains landscape, she was no romantic. She could be equally as honest in her
depiction of a West Texas sandstorm as she is of springtime greening.
Tamzen watches with her family as a "red, unnatural light came down
around them," and the sun became a "red, burned-out disc, as flat as a
dollar." Only just arrived from East Texas, Tamzen says as she witnesses
this sudden change of weather for the first time, "It's like the end of
the world" (141). No one who has experienced West Texas sandstorms
will disagree.

RELIGION

Front-porch storytelling and, as Rushing says in her introduction to
Starting from Pyron, "the indelible stamp of place upon the human psyche" (4) influenced plot, development of character, and theme in her
work. Her knowledge and appreciation of the landscape contributed
to the realism of her work, but perhaps the most powerful motivation
for her choice of theme in her fiction originated in knowledge of the
fundamentalist religion governing the lives of many of the Pyron settlers. Rushing said once in an interview she was "not much of a
churchgoer," but adds she was a member of the Methodist Church as
she grew up. Even so, she says, "I'm much interested in the fundamentalist religions" (Shay Bennett 52). Rushing noticed, as an observant
adolescent, that church members' attitudes, influenced by biblical

commands literally interpreted and amended by leaders, led frequently to the bigoted judgments of others and prejudiced rejection of the nonconformists in their community. After she had written *Covenant of Grace*, set in colonial Boston, Rushing compared the colonists to early West Texas farmers, who "were fundamentalists in their religious thinking, but their thoughts and morals were a lot like the puritans." Patrick Bennett, who includes this comment in his *Dallas Morning News* profile of Rushing, observed two "well-thumbed copies of the King James Bible among the reference books on her desk" when he interviewed the writer in her study.

In her last book-length work, *Starting from Pyron*, Rushing explains the doctrines of the most dominant of the three church denominations, which influenced early community attitudes and, finally, theme in her own work. Baptists and Methodists established churches on the Rolling Plains, but the Church of Christ "seems to be," she says, the prevalent religious group in the region. She succinctly summarizes members' beliefs:

> The appeal of the church is in the doctrine that God is altogether knowable, and the teachings of His Son are sufficient, practical, and reasonable. Pyron people like a practical, understandable doctrine. They like simplicity. They have little patience with mysticism and symbolic ritual. (110)

After *The Raincrow* was published, the author was approached by a woman member of this church, who asked her, "Are you one of us?" Rushing explained she was not, but had learned from a friend who belongs to the Church of Christ about the practice of "turning their back," as they do in the novel, and ejecting a church member that leaders consider has committed a sin (P. Bennett).

None of Rushing's fiction is exempt from her pointed criticism of religious bigotry fostered by narrow interpretations of actions as either right or wrong. Usually this theme emphasizes what she often calls "the looks of the thing" morality, which dictates rules of behavior, particularly for girls and women, in a community. But Rushing's strong attachment to her region tempers her response to this influence. Rushing revisited favorite places and interviewed relatives and friends in the region with her photographer cousin before she wrote *Starting from Pyron*, her version of the region's history in which she shares with her readers her strong personal connection to the long-vanished town of Pyron. Rushing, as she has often said, sees significance in the everyday experiences of rural and small-town West Texans, an opinion that A. C. Greene, who provides the book's introduction, once explored in his own memoir, *A Personal Country*. In one of the final chapters, Rushing sums up with relevant detail traits that contemporary Pyron natives living in the community hold in common. Designating their convictions as a legacy handed down from generation to generation in this region, Rushing says the values of present-day citizens are part of "a kind of Pyron syndrome" (132).

Then she assumes a gentler tone to describe what she terms "the strong religious ambience of the community," this time as more a "form of communion with God and nature" and less as church doctrine. This is not a ritualistic worship, however, and Rushing believes goodness for community members is closely associated with the work ethic:

> Morality is of grave concern to the members of the community. The foundation of their moral code is the Ten Commandments, but they can readily recall Paul's commandment to the Thessalonians "that if any do not work, neither should they eat." Nor do they forget an old saw many grew up hearing: the devil makes works for idle hands. (133)

Rushing understands the ambiguity in this "baggage," or inherited religious values, those starting from Pyron carry with them. Community religious practices lead positively to an awareness of neighbors' lives, and neighborliness leads to abundant help when farmers need extra help or when tragedy or sickness strikes. Too often, however, such closeness results in gossiping and supposition based on the appearance of a citizen's activities. For Rushing these insular early communities in her native region soon acquired, as she observes, "a touch of xenophobia" (134–35).

READING AND LITERATURE

Knowledge of history, place, and community mores enrich Rushing's fiction, but her lifelong love of reading, particularly the classics, also enlivens style in her fiction. Rushing's writing thrives on literary allusion. As a reader and scholar, she is adept at incorporating references to both books and poetry into her stories. No cowboy in a traditional Western lives in a dugout lined with bookshelves, but Rushing chooses this detail to depict an educated cowboy, counter to the traditional notion that early ranch hands often had little education. In a novel reversing traditional roles, Arthur Field, the English cowpoke who treasures his books in *Tamzen,* passes his free evenings reading Tennyson's *Idylls of the King* with Tamzen and her sister and brother, Lutie and Dan. Books are also a passion for young John Carlile in *Walnut Grove*, who cherishes his copy of *Robinson Crusoe* and studies Latin and Greek with the itinerant scholar Sam Flowers, hoping to learn more about Thermopylae, Gaul's three parts, Herodotus, and Homer, subjects he had heard about from Mr. Valentine, his early teacher (201).

One of Rushing's most effective uses of literary allusion is her reference to Tolstoy's *Anna Karenina* as a strategy for character revelation and implicit theme in *Winds of Blame*. Miss Lona has encouraged her student, the knowledge-hungry Isabel, to read *Anna Karenina* at school, because she knows Harvey Doane will not allow the book in his house. Isabel is struck by the relevance of the opening lines to her own situation: "All happy families are alike, but each unhappy family is unhappy in its own way." Isabel ponders several times and at length the nature of unhappiness in families and how wickedness is punished. After her father's murder and her brother Burnie's suicide, Isabel, bereft and exhausted, thinks once again of the question that both this book and her own situation has inspired, "Where does evil come from, and once it establishes itself in a family, can there ever be an end to it?" (282).

In Rushing's novels, references to other familiar works are numerous. She speaks of Fenimore Cooper's works, *Jane Eyre*, *Oedipus the King*, and Walt Whitman's poetry. The title *Winds of Blame* originates in a quotation from *Hamlet*, and the novel's theme is amplified in the epigraph introducing the narrative:

> And for his death no wind of blame shall breathe,
> But even his mother shall uncharge the practice,
> And call it accident. (*Hamlet*, IV, vii)

Mary Dove, as a modern version of the Adam and Eve story, reflects the author's knowledge of Milton's epic account of their dismissal from the Garden of Eden in *Paradise Lost*. Even Brother Michael, like Milton's Angel Michael, escorts the young couple out of their paradise.

For one of the few writers who conveys life on this treeless prairie and in the rough Breaks of West Texas imaginatively, the "baggage" she has acquired from her connections with folk culture, landscape, and local religious beliefs has enabled Rushing to produce fiction that provides insight into the lives and history of people she considers unique. For the re-creation of her native culture, Rushing depends as well on book knowledge, which eventually led to her graduate degrees as well as to her cultural understanding and inspiration for the creation of theme in her fiction.

Themes

With a heritage she appreciates and understands, Rushing was equipped from the beginning of her career to discipline plot and characterization with strong themes and recurring motifs. In several of her novels, the differences in the lifestyles Rushing had experienced or observed on the geographical divide where she lived become pivotal to plot. The author recognized that ranchers' philosophy for living good lives differed greatly from the farmers' rules for living well.

Another obvious thematic thread in her fiction reveals Rushing's understanding and advocacy of women's roles in her native region. Women, who in Rushing's plots are portrayed as "moving forces" in the establishment of civilization on the Rolling Plains, have several characteristics in common. In retrospect, Rushing recognized that the family matriarch as a "moving force" in the home and the community had assumed the strength of motif in most of her fiction.

The most prevalent of the writer's more obvious themes examines the plight of the intellectual in a provincial, conformist society. The resulting religious bigotry and racial prejudice surface to set in motion events resulting in sometimes tragic consequences. To counter the harshness of such community judgments or to cope with unexpressed longing, characters often seek escape, consolation, and even spiritual comfort in the natural world. Rushing explores her own relationship to nature when she remembers her grandfather's declaration that rain won't come up against the moon:

> Remembering and pondering these words, I still seemed
> to sense a meaning in them just beyond the ordinary
> rational thought. I reached for it and caught some hint
> that it had to do with the rhythms of nature—that people
> who live close to the earth and keep aware of the sky find
> a kind of acceptance and understanding of life and death

denied to those who live unaware of the natural world
around them. (*Against the Moon*, reprint, viii)

TWO WEST TEXAS CULTURES

Much of Rushing's fiction reflects her awareness of how separate cultures have developed on the Rolling Plains, where the rough Breaks
proved most viable for cattle raising and the adjoining prairie land
encouraged establishment of cotton farms. In *Starting from Pyron*,
Rushing describes the obvious and accepted differences between
ranchers' and farmers' goals and attitudes, which she explored more
fully in her third novel, *Tamzen*.

Ironically it was a rancher, Bob Pyron, for whom the "town-that-
wanted-to-be" was named. This generous cattleman provided the first
school in the dugout basement under his ranch house kitchen and
donated three acres of land bordering the prairie "expressly for the
purpose of burials with the understanding that there would be no
charge for burial plot and that the people of the community would
take care of the graves" (*Pyron* 140). Rushing adds that "Bob Pyron
was a public-spirited man who contributed considerably toward the
building of the community, but I have never heard anything to suggest
that his family belonged to this community in the same way as the
farm families and the tradesmen who served them" (11).

Such separateness of cultures was evident, as well, in her paternal
grandparents' relationship with their rancher neighbor, Captain Linn
and his wife and daughter. The two families were cordial in passing
but never exchanged visits, nor did ranchers' families join farmers at
Sunday dinner tables, where, after services, churchgoers gathered
regularly in friends' homes for fellowship and the exchange of news.
In her novels reflecting the early history of the region, *Mary Dove,
Walnut Grove,* and *Tamzen*, Rushing provides insight into this social
disjunction.

In *Mary Dove,* the cowboy Red Jones finds his choice between the
contrasting values of the ranching and farming cultures a source of

conflict. His cowpoke friend Jack assures Red that the freedom they experience as Bar Diamond Ranch hands precludes both romantic and religious attachments. Brother Michael, the preacher serving the camping settlers, expresses urgent hope that Red will become a Christian and join the church the early settlers on the prairie plan to establish. Red's dilemma becomes Rushing's theme as she examines the true nature of good and evil, freedom and repression, in this story of a love affair between the mulatto girl and the red-headed cowboy.

In *Walnut Grove*, with the subtle irony characteristic of Rushing's style, the writer shows a standoffish rancher's dependence on the savvy of a cotton farmer's son for a solution to a long-standing mystery. John Carlile at last finds the source of the moving light he and his friends have witnessed periodically in the Breaks as they camp on the edge of the ranch land. Discovering cattle rustlers use the light to signal each other during their roundup of rancher Captain Keith's cattle, John reports his discovery to the cattleman; and with the reward Keith has promised, the young cotton farmer turned bounty hunter decides to reject both farming and ranching and leave for college.

The reversal in the traditional rancher-farmer relationship surfaces as the major theme in *Tamzen*. Not only does a young woman homesteader become the central figure in a free-range cattleman and homesteader feud, but her adversary, Turk Bascom, learns his usual forceful acquisition of whatever he desires impresses Tamzen not at all. Rather than developing as plot the expected capitulation of the homesteader to an avaricious and desirous rancher, Rushing creates a narrative one critic, Becky Matthews, has called the "un-Western." Eventually the cowboy Arthur Field, whom Tamzen will marry, agrees to relinquish his dream of becoming a rancher and chooses instead to become a farmer on Tamzen's homestead.

Rushing often said the cycles in the history of her region intrigued her. She explains why: "My grandparents were among the first of the farming people in that area; the ranchers had come some twenty years earlier, while the buffalo hunters were still having a little trouble with Indians. I am fascinated by the way history is compressed in my home region" (Elder 126). In at least five of her novels, the author introduces as the theme the ambivalence of her own response to this region of contrasts in landscape and lifestyle. For Rushing, both positive and negative elements exist in the practice of either vocation. Her fiction reflects the compromises the region's settlers accepted, although sometimes reluctantly, and consequently often refutes the tired formula of the traditional Western, where ranchers usually dominated when homesteaders showed up to claim the free range the cowmen had so long enjoyed.

ROLE OF WOMEN

One of Rushing's most substantial contributions to the literature of the West is her spirited portrayal of women as protagonists who provide a woman's perspective on Western history. Dorothy Scarborough attempted a depiction of how women responded to life in this same region when in *The Wind* (1925) she created a Southern belle unable to cope with the harsh realities she experienced on a hardscrabble ranch near Sweetwater, where the Rolling Plains of Rushing's novels begins. In this novel, Scarborough also characterizes a tough ranch wife who lacks compassion, but Rushing sees the woman's role differently three decades later. For Rushing, some women who came to the too-late frontier were unable to cope, to be sure; and she is honest in her description of young women like Lutie and Ellie in *Tamzen*, who find isolation on the dusty prairie almost unbearable. But most of her women narrators exhibit both determination and ingenuity as they build homes and raise families in the often hostile environment.

The strong women in Rushing's novels most often demonstrate the characteristics of the recurring character in her novels that she belatedly recognized as the Grandmother of West Texas. The author's variations on this template create distinctive women characters, whose influence is felt community-wide. Rushing once said these strong-minded women were "a 'mixed blessing' for future generations." Ariel Peugh, who recorded this comment in a discussion of the dominant figures in Rushing's fiction with the writer, says the Grandmother of West Texas may be either a romantic grandmother or a sanctimonious grandmother. The first is the moving force Rushing has described her as being. Both community and family depend upon her for guidance and support. The second, usually of a subsequent generation among the settlers, becomes obsessed with community morality and the appearance of wrong doing, the "looks-of-the-thing" as Rushing phrases the hypocritical judgments of these trouble makers in her novels (Peugh 121).

"LOOKS-OF-THE-THING" MORALITY AND ANTI-INTELLECTUALISM

This characteristic of judging others superficially by appearance, soon obvious in Rushing's first novel, *Walnut Grove,* provides motivation for characters' responses as well as for much of what occurs in the narrative. The measurement of moral uprightness by judging appearance is a prevalent theme often leading to damaging results in all of Rushing's novels. The hypocrisy innate in this measure of a person's goodness fuels controversy and alienates truth seekers in her works. Suspicion and ostracism of the outsider or nonconformist, resulting from the bigotry spawned by superficial judgment of actions, logically follows as a motif in Rushing's fiction. Intellectually gifted, Jane Gilmore Rushing rarely mentioned her educational accomplishments; but she was often uneasy with the anti-intellectualism she experienced, even in Pyron, as a child who loved books. Later after settling in Lubbock, she felt Texas Tech professors and the few writers spawned on the High Plains rarely gained any recognition from the local media. She told Pat Bennett in 1982 that "historically, the daily newspaper here has done a lot to foster anti-intellectualism. The editorial page used to talk rather disparagingly about 'long-haired professors' back when

most persons weren't long-haired. Lubbock is a university town of
200,000, and there is no locally written book review in the paper" (P.
Bennett).

Never one to ignore the negatives in a society that had nurtured
her imagination and her ambitions, Rushing understood, nevertheless, that intellectual growth was not a priority for most of her peers
in the community. She reveals her early awareness of being an outsider
in her home region with her admission that she identifies most
closely with the characters John Carlile in *Walnut Grove*, who longs to
escape the provincialism of his home region, and Gail Messenger in
The Raincrow, who as college professor comes back to this region as
a stranger seeking to find answers to personal problems as well as
to why she left her birthplace so abruptly as a young woman
(Peugh 154).

In *Walnut Grove*, although John Carlile had lived in the region all of
his life, his love of reading and his questioning spirit make his father
uneasy and his brother Frank hostile, especially when he tells Frank,
"[A]ll my life I've wanted to learn more than I ever had a chance to
learn at Walnut Grove, and I'm not giving up my chance now" (207).
What Frank resents is John's friendship with the itinerant teacher, Sam
Flowers, who has introduced John to the classics. Like John, at least one
character in most of Rushing's novels yearns for knowledge not easily
attainable in his or her present circumstances. Isabel, the protagonist in
Winds of Blame, longs for time and opportunity to learn, but hides her
loaned copy of *Anna Karenina* from her brutal father, who allows nothing but the Bible in his household. When the gypsies Raven Concolorcorvo and her musician son John drive in to camp near the springs
in "Wayfaring Strangers," Perdue Springs citizens express great unease
at the unannounced arrival of the newcomers, those "Dagos" who
"talked funny" and furthermore "looked funny." Only the girl Rosie
Fargo sees their arrival as her means of escape from poverty to the
world of song and dance she hungers to sample. The native with intellectual and artistic aspirations who invites criticism and longs for

escape and the outsider who brings new ideas and different values into close-knit societies such as Walnut Grove and Perdue Springs are implicit as the theme in much of Rushing's fiction.

Linked with the restlessness of those who feel out of place in the environment they live in, the outsider may be a native who strives for different goals from the expected or the newcomer who seems bent on seeking truth behind appearance, but who always strives for individual freedom.

Mr. Godwin assures young John Carlile that freedom is "[w]orth anything in the world . . . if you know what to do with it" (*Walnut Grove* 250). For Tamzen, homesteading her own land offers an independence she aims to preserve. She thinks of her freedom as "a real house to go home to, with a bedstead and mattress made up with fresh laundered sheets and pillow cases" (317). For the early settlers, owning land and their own home represented the ultimate freedom. In Rushing's fiction, the protagonist's search for freedom of spirit and intellect becomes a major element of whatever theme she chooses to develop.

Influenced by the region's folklore, her family's stories, her love of books, and her concept of regional religious practices, Rushing shapes her fiction around themes reflecting her understanding of a region she perceives as worthy of a novelist's search for meaning in the lives of those who settled one of Texas's last frontiers.

Chapter 3

THE WALNUT GROVE NOVELS
AS FICTIVE HISTORY

RUSHING'S PUBLISHING CAREER began in an unexpected way. Once she had decided to concentrate on her writing, she admits she was still intimidated by the notion she could publish a novel. Although she had tentatively started writing *Walnut Grove,* her first submission to a publisher was her short story "Against the Moon." The fiction editor of *Ladies Home Journal* rejected the story, saying it was not the kind of fiction usually published in a women's magazine. Rushing said she sensed the editor was implying there was something unsuitable in the story; but her critic failed to elaborate, although she did suggest the short story sounded more like a first chapter of a novel.

Then, without hesitation, when Rushing's husband Jay brought to her attention an announcement of the Emily Clark Balch short-story competition he had found posted on his department bulletin board, she sent "Against the Moon" as her entry in the contest. She was surprised when she eventually learned she had won second prize in the contest. Soon several publishers requested submission of any novel she might have in manuscript. Rushing quickly finished *Walnut Grove.* Doubleday accepted the novel if she was willing to revise it. Her husband Jay reports that with the assistance of Rushing's editor, Ellen Roberts, the manuscript was soon ready for publication (Letter to the author, August 11, 1998).

Walnut Grove (1964)

In her introduction to the 1992 reprint of *Walnut Grove*, the author points out that the fictional community has much in common with Pyron, both in its landscape and its citizens. Furthermore, the story itself follows closely the early life of her father. In her note to the reader at the beginning of "Recollections of a West Texas Boyhood," Rushing says *Walnut Grove* was based on the stories recorded here. Narrated in first person, this personal history of one pioneer family's early activities mirrors in most cases the history of most of the early settlers. "Recollections" narrates the stories of the Gilmore family's arrival in the region, establishment of schools and churches, and their social life. The coming of the railroad and the grand celebration greeting its arrival, as vividly described by Rushing's father, becomes the crucial time of decision for John Carlile in *Walnut Grove*. In *Starting from Pyron*, Rushing calls the coming of the railroad "almost as though a mighty river had begun to flow through the land" (31).

But the railroad did not bring the prosperity the community had anticipated. Clyde Gilmore candidly shares his memories of how the expected development of a prosperous town did not follow what early settlers remembered as "the most spectacular event" most had ever experienced:

> You might say it was the end as well as the beginning.
> The store buildings stood empty. The hotel became a shell
> of a building that sometimes sheltered a transient family
> looking for a roof. Before long everything that was a
> reminder of the town of Pyron had disappeared except
> for the store in its new location and the isolated water
> tank. The grass grew over broken sidewalks. The town lots
> became pastureland and were finally plowed up into

fields. . . . If we woke in the night and heard a lonesome
whistle down in Linn Hollow, it brought back the most
exciting memories of our lifetime and roused in us
dreams that we could never have dreamed before the railroad came. (86)

Mabel Adams Gilmore's Appendix I to Clyde's account briefly
tells some of her own story. Of particular interest in this account are
descriptions of the early houses that challenged her mother and other
stalwart pioneer women, who made their families comfortable in
flimsy box-and-strip, two-room houses with dirt-floored, lean-to
kitchens as they fought regular battles with wind and sand. Despite
early hardship, the family was literate and enjoyed books. For a short
while, the family lived in an old ranch house during the construction
of their new house in Pyron. Rushing's mother wrote, "Papa read to
us a lot at night while we lived at the Ranch—we would gather
around the fireplace after work was 'done up' and he would read
Robinson Crusoe because that was the book we had. I can remember
once in a while, he would read a Sherlock Holmes story."

Despite her reliance for material on these adventures of her parents as they grew up in Pyron, Rushing says that the protagonist is
"altogether the boy I made up out of my own head." Nevertheless,
John Carlile, barely six years old in the opening scenes of *Walnut
Grove*, experiences many of the same perceptions of this new country
as those of young Clyde Gilmore upon his arrival in 1897. The phases
of John's life are presented in three sections, simply titled "The Little
Boy," "The Big Boy," and "The Young Man." Significantly, this progression of John's life encompasses the cycles of Walnut Grove's development into what area citizens, who gather at the novel's conclusion
to celebrate the coming of the railroad, believe will be a vital town.
Destined to abandon the town he believes is corrupted by its citizens'
double moral vision, John Carlile recognizes even as an inexperienced
youth that judging success by appearance in no way reveals the truth

of a town's values and culture. He has acquired uncommon wisdom for a nineteen-year-old.

"The Little Boy" opens with John's memories of his first impressions as he peers out of a covered wagon following the wagon tracks of other pioneer families through the mesquite-covered land that would become his country. John's descriptions of the images he remembers from this first time he traveled the road into the community from the east remain in his consciousness as "the way he always remembered it." A perceptive child, he recalls first the huge mesquite trees. Rushing, whose response to color is that of an artist, creates one of the dominant images in this novel's setting as seen through the eyes of this observant child as he remembers the mesquites:

> They had belonged to the land a long time: branches
> reaching up to make a mark on the sky had twisted back
> downward to touch the earth again. The thin lacy leaves
> were still green, but the slanting sunlight turned them
> glinty gray, like the metal of a fresh-sharpened plow. The
> leaves and grass were colorless pale, and the tree trunks
> and branches were colorless dark, so that the day was the
> color of deep blue October sky as they traveled the last
> mile on the way to the new place. (3)

With his older brother Frank and sister Alice, John soon feels at home in this land so different from the East Texas farm they have left behind. For the child, memories of early images mark the beginning of his life, although John would come to know some of his family's history "back yonder" in East Texas, when his paternal grandmother arrives and singles out this grandchild as special. Grandma Carlile introduces for the first time in this novel the grandmother figure, later to appear in *Against the Moon, The Raincrow,* and "Wayfaring Strangers." What these wise old women each have in common is an uncommon understanding of their grandchildren.

Grandma Carlile soon demonstrates that she believes John has a special intelligence not obvious in others around her. When she arrives, she hugs all of the children, but she whispers to John, "We'll have a lot to talk about when we have some time to ourselves." Later, she asks questions John did not expect. These were not the usual queries into whether he had been a good boy, but questions that begin: "But tell me about your trip. How did it feel to ride all that way in a covered wagon?" The wise grandmother has appealed to the little boy's imagination. John begins thinking about just how to answer such a question. He remembers he felt as snug under the wagon sheet as "a rabbit in a hollow log." When he shows her the child's saddle he has acquired from its owner with the trade of a knife, he is surprised when his grandmother can't tell him whether it is a good trade or not. Grown-ups usually responded as though they knew all the answers. The uncertainty that he may have made a bad trade has been bothering the six-year-old, and he admits to his grandmother that his dad laughed when he learned of the swap. Grandma is honest and says she doesn't know much about saddles and knives, but she adds, "Maybe he laughed because he was surprised you had made such a good trade." To John, this "frankness in a grown person was astounding and disarming" (20–21).

Soon the sensitive child has another question to puzzle over. A description of the family's first Christmas in West Texas begins with the Carliles' neighbor, Mr. Godwin, joining John and his father as they drive out to cut a big cedar tree for the Christmas celebration at the New Hope schoolhouse. Although for John the trip is a gala occasion, he senses that Mr. Godwin's recollection of going for a Christmas tree in the Old States irritates his father. Mr. Godwin recalls the great tall pine tree he and half dozen other men, "laughing and hollering" finally brought in. When Mr. Godwin tells John it was for "a great big house, with ceilings so high they didn't even have to top the tree to set it up in the front hall," John wants to know what kind of a house this was. His father jerks the team to a stop. "Hush, no more of that now," he commands. For John, the scolding seemed to be not only for him but for Mr. Godwin (25).

John would learn much later how Mr. Godwin's role in the settlement's life reflected the community's double standard in moral judgment where appearance always wins out over the truth. Mr. Godwin, although accepted as white by his neighbors, has facial features that seem incongruous with Anglo features. He acts as the community advisor, however, and the settlers turn to him both for advice and for assistance during harvest time. John remembers Mr. Godwin as a "heavy, stooped man with a full-face, gray beard, and dark sunken eyes" (5). Because of Mr. Godwin's availability as a helpful and wise neighbor, John wonders why his father would disapprove of Mr. Godwin's tale telling. The answer gradually becomes apparent as John grows up and finally comprehends that Walnut Grove settlers refuse to recognize Mr. Godwin as African American.

Soon after John's first Christmas party at New Hope, a school located some miles from many of the settlement's children, John's father spearheads a request for a new school district. In a short while, the men of the community go to work constructing a new school building. Grandma Carlile is indirectly responsible for naming the school, and eventually the town, Walnut Grove, an improbable name in a land where only persistent mesquite trees grow. Walnut Grove was the name of Grandma's home "back yonder" in Tennessee. She tries to explain to John the significance of her memories of Walnut Grove, an elegant book-filled house destroyed during the Civil War. She describes her father's joining the "army of freedom" and being "taken away" by men who burned their home. She never saw her father again.

Even though her own son laughs at her notion that the school should be named Walnut Grove, Grandma Carlile is unmoved. She smiles, orders a dozen walnut trees, and supervises their planting around the new school building. John has treasured her stories of the first Walnut Grove, and "he knew too, somehow, that she had planted these trees for him" (33–34). Only three of the trees live; but when his

ailing Grandma asks him in the fall if the trees are still there, he assures
her that they are, believing his lie is an act of love.

Grandma lives long enough to comfort John one more time.
When he forgets to feed his old pony Scissortail and finds his pet dead
the next morning, he is sure he caused the death. Grandma says, "Oh
John, don't always care so much. . . . [B]elieve me, you didn't make
him die. Animals die, people die, in the Lord's good time." Then the
child knows intuitively that soon his grandmother will die too. She
admits this is so, but reassures him, urging him to remember that "[i]t
comes in love, John, it all comes in love" (42–43). The events leading
up to Grandma Carlile's death follow closely Clyde Gilmore's recollections of his own grandmother's last days. After John and his brother
spend the night in a neighbor's dugout, a necessary arrangement after
relatives begin to arrive to await Grandma's death, John knows when
he walks into the quiet house the next morning that his grandmother
has died.

The walnut grove survives only a little longer than Grandma does.
Only one hardy sapling stands through the school's third year. Soon
there are several prosperous cotton farms surrounding the school, a
tabernacle open to all denominations, a graveyard, and much talk of
bringing a railroad to the community now known as Walnut Grove, a
name no longer connected to its origins by most citizens. When the
school is moved to the Walnut Grove town site, John makes sure the
surviving tree is transplanted to become a scrawny shade in front of
the building. Only he seems to remember why those with high hopes
for development of a prosperous town still call it Walnut Grove. It's
just a name, as one citizen points out.

When John begins school, he once again has a champion like
Grandma in the person of Old Man Valentine, his quiet, unimpressive
teacher. John does not at first recognize that Mr. Valentine is particularly interested in his progress as a scholar. Mostly, the students make
Mr. Valentine the butt of their practical jokes. John, however, soon
wins his schoolmates' scorn by befriending his teacher. Conforming

to the examples set by the bullies in the school is not an option for John. He knows that "[y]ou just couldn't come out openly on the teacher's side" without censure by his peers, but he cannot join the others in loading Mr. Valentine's desk with bitterweed bouquets. The joke backfires with consequences not favorable to the jokers (53–54).

Earlier, after Grandma Carlile begins teaching him to read, John yearns for access to more books than are available in this isolated community. Few know Dr. Jim Matthiessen's history, but John's family calls him to take care of Grandma after her stroke. When John visits the doctor with his father, he is mesmerized by the piles of books stacked in the physician's open trunk. Dr. Matthiessen sees the boy's interest and gives him a book, although John cannot in truth read well enough to enjoy it. Later, he tells Mr. Valentine about this book with a title he cannot pronounce. He can write the title, however, and his teacher assures him that he now has the skills to read *Robinson Crusoe*. His teacher's approval of his reading, even at school all day, reassures John that liking books does not make him a misfit among those who value physical over mental achievement as his father does.

As he grows intellectually and physically, John becomes aware, as the section on "The Big Boy" begins, that in comparison to his brother Frank, he does not measure up to his father's standards for demonstrating his manhood. Young men on the verge of adulthood should be more interested in farming than books. John does what he is expected to do on the farm, but he has discovered what he thinks of as his "signal rock." He often wanders off to Slab Rock Hill, as he and his friends call it, where he can see far to the east across the Breaks. After dark comes, the boys often see what they begin to call "the Light" moving low like a disembodied lantern. The moving light intrigues and beckons the boys of the community, particularly John, during camp outs. For four years, they see the light off and on. Occasionally they ride their horses down into the Breaks aiming to solve this mystery, but they give up the search as dawn breaks. John later learns that the light provides signals between cattle rustlers rounding

up Captain Keith's herds. John's discovery symbolically becomes the
beginning of his break for freedom.

Meanwhile, Mr. Godwin becomes John's close friend. An early
settler on whom the community depends for both friendship and
spiritual guidance, Mr. Godwin is "like the road and the mesquite pasture." He has always been a part of John's life. It is Mr. Godwin who
relates much of the area's early history for curious young John. The
boy has noticed as they talk and work together that Mr. Godwin
responds differently to some of the everyday experiences in the community. For one thing, when John works for Mr. Godwin, helping a
neighbor as was the custom, the old farmer pays him, sometimes only
a nickel or a dime in lean times, but John remembers he always pays.
None of the other farmers do this, expecting to repay the boys' time
working for them by helping their father with his harvest and farm
work when they are needed.

Like John, Mr. Godwin notices the natural life around him. Surprising John while he is burning brush one spring day, Mr. Godwin in
his deep, rich voice teases him, "If you don't mind out, laziness'll kill
you!" Then he explains to the embarrassed boy that he is just repeat-
ing the warning of the "fee-larks," the settlers' vernacular name for the
"field lark." He adds, "Least that's what I used to hear back in the Old
States" (87). Mr. Godwin assures John, embarrassed to be caught sitting, that watching the burning brush from his seat on the ground is
just as good as standing. As they watch the fire together, they talk.
John finds his friend's presence comforting, and he recognizes that
Mr. Godwin's words "made him feel as if he had been there a long
time—like Mr. Godwin and the field larks—as if he belonged to the
country, as they did, would go on, as they had, past any shortcoming
or catastrophes, past even the longest drouth" (88).

The boy quietly listens to Mr. Godwin tell about the early days in
the region when he came in as a buffalo hunter. When the rancher
Captain Keith rides up on his big star-faced bay, the tale-telling ses-

sion ends while they listen to the cattleman's complaints that the con-
tinuous theft of his cattle puzzles him. He hastily assures his listeners
he is not suspicious of his neighbors because they have no pastures to
hold the stolen stock.

After the rancher leaves, Mr. Godwin listens as John expresses his
disapproval of impinging on good ranch land to raise cotton. He
regrets his father's clearing their pasture land for cotton, even though
the drouth seems endless. Mr. Godwin accepts the inevitable. He
knows rains will finally come and predicts, "This is gonna be cotton
country, John, and you can't help it, and I can't. I like it the way it is—
I liked it the way it was in the beginning—but you can't help yourself, things change. Cotton's going to be growing all over the Divide"
(89–90). John retorts that he does not like that idea. Later, as he contemplates his father's aim to move back to East Texas if rain does not
soon come, he rides out to the Breaks on his horse Pancho, vowing
that "Pa can't take me back." John's thoughts as he looks across the
low hills reveals his romantic notions of the adventures this land
offers, but the boy's imagination is fueled by his longing for a freedom
he never feels working on a cotton farm. As he sits on Slab Rock Hill,
he again swears never to leave this country:

> He stepped off his horse, kicking up clouds of dust from
> dead weeds, touched the carved rock, made a sign on his
> forehead, and rode on again. He was Lone Eagle, the
> blood of Cherokees ran in his veins, and now that was all
> that mattered. Nobody knew him; he rode alone, he
> knew the trails of rabbits and possums, he had the com-
> panionship of ancient hunters, he felt the meaning of
> wind and clouds. He rode down into the Hollow, turned
> toward the place where buffalo used to water. (98)

A gang of friends ride up then and interrupts John's reverie. Clearly for an adolescent, John senses, at least subconsciously, what Rushing herself expresses in her essays. Cotton farming will change the plains landscape forever.

John's friendship with Mr. Godwin continues to flourish. Then one Sunday the boy goes to church with his family with a feeling of foreboding. They sing old familiar hymns that John likes: "Showers of Blessings," "There Is a Fountain," and "Come Ye Sinners." When the preacher finishes his sermon, Mr. Godwin rises to testify. He had done so before, but this time his eyes are fierce and "his thick grizzled beard seemed alive." Mr. Godwin tells the congregation he has things on his heart he must share. In his mellow, musical voice, Mr. Godwin begins, "Oh, brothahs and sistahs." Then he seems on the verge of confessing what he proclaims as "[s]uch wickedness I done." His impassioned speech is cut short when the tormented man breaks off to weep. John's father quietly guides him from the church. What puzzles John is the dialect Mr. Godwin seems to have slipped into unconsciously. John remembers he had heard old people pronounce their words in the same fashion, but he had never heard Mr. Godwin speak that way.

John puzzles over Mr. Godwin's actions, and then black railroad construction workers move into Mulberry Hollow in the Breaks, where the company builds a temporary settlement for them. John observes that Walnut Grove citizens accept the black workers, isolated in the Breaks, on a temporary basis. Community attitudes are mixtures of curiosity, prejudice, and revulsion. Finally, after selling rabbits to the blacks and talking with them, John recognizes that his good friend and confidante Mr. Godwin is black as well. The person who verifies this truth is Sam Flowers, an itinerant professor, who tutors John, an eager student. Sam sees clearly as a perceptive outsider that it is the "looks-of-the-thing" that matters in Walnut Grove. A sojourner briefly in the town, Flowers says it is obvious to him that everybody knows that Mr. Godwin is partly black, but as he has observed, "as soon as you start to talk to people around here, . . . everybody knows he has Negro blood but won't admit it. They think as long as they don't say it, it's not true; but if they ever admitted it he'd have to leave the country" (215).

When Flowers urges John to leave Walnut Grove, John balks. This is his home. He belongs in Walnut Grove, he protests. But when he learns his father is plotting to rid Walnut Grove of Sam Flowers's influence, John realizes he needs to do some thinking. He needs to find a quiet place. He heads for Slab Rock Hill. When he once again sees the now mythical light out in the Breaks, he decides to solve the mystery once and for all. He catches the light bearers, cattle thieves in the act of stealing Captain Keith's cows, and turns them over to the Captain. With the thousand-dollar reward the rancher gives him, John now has money to leave for the university at Austin. Feeling like the man his father has always wanted him to be, he decides instead that he will buy land with his money and settle down with Mary Bailey, the storekeeper's daughter. On the day when the community celebrates the railroad's completion and the town site's opening, however, John admits finally that Sam Flowers has been right about the town. He knows he must leave Walnut Grove.

On that hot summer day in 1910, all of the region's citizens gathered in a festive mood to celebrate the arrival of the first train and to open the town site. John's experiences that day lead to his final decision to break his engagement to Mary Bailey. Already Mr. Godwin has advised John, "Don't think about what anybody wants, not even what you want yourself, but only what you know in your heart" (240). John is shocked and grieved then to discover the city fathers have cut down the remaining walnut tree in front of the schoolhouse to make room for a sidewalk. The irony, of course, is that the town will become officially Walnut Grove on that day. John mourns as he paces the school yard. He declares to himself that "[h]e would make them call it—oh, anything—Idiotville. Well, he would call it that. He would get away from it on the first train that came whistling through, as soon as he got his money from Captain Keith, and the rest of his life, if he thought of it, he would call it Idiotville" (243).

Later, when John visits for the last time with Mr. Godwin, his friend tells him finally the story of how, as an ex-slave, he came to this region to live as a free man. He also admits he killed a white man to gain his freedom. He declares that freedom, if you know how to use it, is your most important possession. He continues that for him freedom has meant owning a farm, working hard for his family, and having the respect of other hardworking men. He adds, "And I reckon I'd do the same again, though I never had much family, and I've had to live all of my days in fear of being found out . . . for that's the kind of sin not forgive on this earth" (250).

After advising John to follow his heart and leave town, they walk to the Baileys for supper. As they walk, they pass the newly erected town sign, which Frank has most likely erected. Under the town name, in the community's accepted colloquial language, is printed the message that blacks will not be allowed in Walnut Grove after sundown. When John stands looking at the sign with his good friend, he realizes he finally has certain knowledge of his alienation from Walnut Grove. He knows, too, that Mr. Godwin need have no fear of being found out. Mr. Godwin's neighbors know he is mulatto; but as Sam Flowers has told him, if they don't allow themselves to acknowledge that truth, then they can both enjoy Mr. Godwin's contributions to church and community life and hold tight to their prejudices.

Rushing once commented that her readers often asked her if she planned to write anymore about John Carlile after he left Walnut Grove to attend college in Austin. She told Pat Bennett she thought maybe he became either Walter Prescott Webb or William Curry Holden (both noted Texas historians).

Because Rushing includes the account of the community's school Christmas celebration in *Walnut Grove,* this first novel enjoyed what Rushing has called "a second life." When *Redbook* decided to feature Texas in their Christmas issue in 1977, the editor of the popular magazine asked Rushing to submit a Christmas short story. Rushing had no story to send, but she asked her editor at Doubleday to send a copy of *Walnut Grove* to the periodical. Her thought was that *Redbook* might wish to excerpt the account of the community Christmas celebration. The periodical immediately sent Rushing the good news that they would like to reprint the complete book in their December issue (Elder 119). Remarkably, as a *Redbook* novel, *Walnut Grove* attracted wide readership once again, thirteen years after its initial publication in 1964. In 1992 the novel was published as a university press reprint.

In this first novel, the author questions relentlessly the standards by which Walnut Grove citizens judge others and conduct their own lives. Neighborly, religious, hardworking, even courageous, these tough frontier dwellers nevertheless are willing to allow their judgment of others and their own standards of conduct to be based almost exclusively on appearance. Rather than make an effort to discern the truth of their experiences, it is much more comfortable to ignore the obvious when the truth would disturb the status quo, a recurring motif in Rushing's fiction. Her next novel, *Against the Moon*, examines how denial of the truth comes close to wrecking family unity.

Against the Moon (1968)

Walnut Grove traces early regional history through the first decade of the twentieth century. In *Against the Moon,* Rushing narrows her focus. Her second novel is based on one remembered event, presents the lives of one extended family, and takes place in one summer month of 1960. Despite its limited setting and time, this work reflects a native's insight into the dynamics of a West Texas family gathered to await the matriarch's death.

Matriarch seems not quite the label for the tiny grandmother whose life is obviously almost over when the novel begins; but Granny Albright's influence, the reader soon realizes, will live on long after her death. Although his understanding Grandma perceives that six-year-old John Carlile has great potential for abundant living in *Walnut Grove*, she dies soon after her arrival in West Texas. In *Against the Moon,* Rushing introduces for the first time the fully developed grandmother figure the author would eventually identify as the Grandmother of West Texas, who appears with variations in most of her works. Lying comatose, Granny Albright still influences family memories and relationships. Flashbacks on crucial events in Granny Albright's long life become a catalyst in the search for a solution to conflict in the lives of three Albright women representing the next three generations.

In her discussion of the origins of both the short story "Against the Moon" and the novel in her introduction to the 1999 reprint of *Against the Moon*, Rushing discusses the source of her inspiration for both works. As she reconstructs her memory of her grandfather's prediction that thunderstorms never occur during the moon's waning, the author considers further why her grandfather's words left such a strong impression:

> I reached for [the meaning] and caught some hint that it
> had to do with the rhythms of nature—that people who
> live close to the earth and keep aware of the sky find a
> kind of acceptance and understanding of life and death
> denied to those who live unaware of the natural world
> around them. It began to seem rather wonderful to me
> that this woman had lived to be old and could now lie
> down and die with all her family around her, attending
> her in the last days, waiting with her for the moment to
> come, not separated from it by hospital walls—by special-
> ists they didn't know and technology they didn't under-
> stand. (viii)

After the short story "Against the Moon," based on these family happenings, won the Emily Clark Balch short story award, Rushing completed revisions on her *Walnut Grove* manuscript and immediately began the novel suggested by events in the short story. Instead of following the advice of a *Ladies Home Journal* editor, Rushing soon realized the best use of the story would be development "by elaboration rather than extension" (*Against the Moon* vii–ix). Rather than a chapter in her novel, the author found the short story would essentially serve as an outline for the novel. She says, "I didn't see the short story as a first chapter; I never had. To me it had always been both the beginning and the end, because whatever the whole story turned out to be, it had to be woven in with the dying of the great-grandmother" (*Against the Moon* viii). In the short story, Granny Albright's life affects only that of Linda Kay, who makes her first mature decision when she assumes responsibility for bathing and dressing Granny after her death. In both works, Granny's final days draw the family home; but in the short story, the "well-rounded teenager" Linda Kay emerges as the only fully developed character.

For the novel, with plot complications already suggested by the short story, Rushing introduces as narrators Maurine, Granny's middle-aged granddaughter; Linda Kay, Maurine's young sister-in-law; and Debora, cousin Howard's troubled adolescent daughter. Both generational and family conflicts among the three and their interaction with Granny Albright's life history through memories of her advice and example increase complexity and meaning in the novel. The plot development depends on examination of events from the third-person point of view of each of the narrators. Granny Albright's influence comes to life principally in Maurine's memory. Her portrayal, however, does not reflect the personality traits, that the author remembers so well, of Great-Grandmother Freeman, who lay dying that summer in 1935. The writer recalled little about this great-grandmother as a person because she died when Rushing was only nine years old. Characterized instead, she says, is "everybody's grandmother," more likely reflecting the characteristics of Jane's Grandma Adams.

The plot of the short story focuses on the bride Linda Kay's

wavering desire to yield to cousin Howard's ardent efforts to seduce
her and her mature decision to reject her would-be seducer on the
day of Granny's dying. On that rainy afternoon, when the long drouth
ends and Granny dies, Linda Kay recognizes her role as a dependable
Albright woman. She rebuffs cousin Howard's advances and compe-
tently prepares Granny's body before burial. Family relationships,
however, receive scant attention in the short story, set in the years of
the Great Depression, even though her development of the initiation
theme announces Rushing's ability to portray characters with dimension and believable motivation.

Development of the longer work, as with *Walnut Grove*, depends
upon family stories to provide color and detail in the narrative,
although Rushing moves the time to the 1960s. According to the
author's introduction to the 1991 reprint of *Against the Moon*, when
members of her family gathered to attend to the dying great-grandmother's needs and to wait together, she remembers that the children
in the family "drifted about the place in little bunches. . . . There were
strange happenings among the adults, too," she says (vi). Most intense
is the memory of her grandfather's voice proclaiming that "a cloud
won't come up against the moon." Rushing continues, "Remembering and pondering those words, I still seemed to sense a meaning in
them just beyond rational thought" (vii–viii). This larger meaning
originates in a closeness to nature these West Texas farmers experienced daily. Implicit in all that Rushing writes is her belief that awareness of the rhythms of nature leads to a stoic acceptance of death.

Children in the novel lead lives independent of supervision by the
busy, preoccupied adults. Debora, reluctantly accepted into the children's games by cousins she barely knows, hears one cousin describe a
way to acquire a new dress: "[I]f you bite a butterfly's head off you'll
get a dress the same color as its wings" (47). Impulsively, Debora bites
the head off a colorful insect, regretting immediately her effort to
prove her courage to her cousins. Rushing admits, in her discussion of
Against the Moon, that Debora's rash action mirrors her own personal

experience with cousins who gathered the summer her Grandma
Freeman died:

> Our grandmother told us anyone that bit off a butterfly's
> head would get a new dress or shirt the color of its wings.
> Surely at no other time in my life would I have done
> such a thing, but I caught a yellow butterfly and bit its
> head off. I felt guilty immediately and still do. But I did
> get a yellow dress that summer. And twenty-five years
> later I remembered the experience so well that I needed
> to write about it. (vi)

Rushing freely incorporates such personal observations and experiences in the first novels she wrote.

In *Against the Moon*, Granny Albright, who has outlived her influence on family decisions when she has the debilitating stroke, leaves
instead memories of her invincibility tempered by her innate understanding of human error. Some of her grandchildren learn to avoid
such error only after painful missteps, despite Granny Albright's
remembered advice and example. Before the dark of the moon arrives
and Granny dies as Cousin Bill has predicted, the lives of the Albright
women have intertwined and led to revelations of family secrets and
conflicts among the relatives. Bobby Joe, the youngest of Mama
Albright's children, just out of high school and just married, has
brought his bride, Linda Kay, to live in the weaning house West Texas
families often provided for newlyweds. Rushing explains the function
of the weaning house in *Starting from Pyron*. Beginning with the early
settlement of the region, farmers customarily provided a two-room
house near the family home and a job on the farm until the newly-
wed son could "get on his feet," as West Texans would have phrased it.
Rushing explains further:

> The custom did not originate with the Depression. It was
> an aspect of frontier life that hung on longer because the

Depression came. Even after World War II it persisted; but
by that time conditions had changed so much that a boy
would never be satisfied very long to live the way his
father lived. He would get a better deal, a better house, or
be off to a job in town. (86-87)

When Rushing visits the relic of one of these little houses, she
observes that where several layers of wallpaper have been torn off she
can see a distinctive pattern in one layer:

> That paper with pink rosebuds and green leaves; it must
> have made the little room seem pretty and new, for some
> hopeful young bride who came to live there. If she had a
> good linoleum rug on the floor and fresh oil cloth for the
> kitchen table, she must have been proud of her house, and
> as well satisfied as most Pyron housewives for she had
> running water and a kitchen sink. (87)

In just such a house, Linda Kay and Bobby Joe have started their
married life. Keeping the little house is not much of a challenge
for Linda Kay, who considers herself, ironically, "a well-rounded
teenager," so she spends part of her day at the Albright house. As the
narrative begins, Linda Kay is shelling peas with her mother-in-law
on Mama Albright's back porch. Her sisters-in-law have assembled to
help, and Granny Albright has joined in. Linda Kay feels a kinship
with the old woman, almost ninety, since neither she nor Granny has
much to say. Then one of the sisters-in-law observes that the shriveled
peas are products of the drouth plaguing the region. Granny startles
them when she laughs and says, "I ain't got so much juice left in me
neither; . . . But I reckon you just take what the good Lord provides, if
it's peas or your own innards" (3). Those were the last words Linda
Kay ever heard Granny say. The next day a stroke stills Granny
Albright's busy little hands, setting into motion the novel's plot.

Before the rains come and Granny dies, the three narrators connect with her presence. Debora, almost twelve and coping with the physical changes adolescence brings, looks to Linda Kay for answers to puzzling questions. Linda Kay, immature and innocent, longs for more attention from her spoiled good ol' boy bridegroom. Maurine, the pragmatic spinster daughter of Mama and Papa Albright, has to deal with painful memories of her own past relationship with her cousin Howard. This womanizing relative stirs up old emotions and heartaches as well as causes problems for all three women protagonists. Maurine, once the favored grandchild of Granny Albright, who has acquired both self-confidence and wisdom since her long-ago affair with Howard, soon believes it is up to her to set the younger Albright women on course and obstruct Howard's devious intentions.

The family gathers on the front porch every evening, under the waning moon, where they reconstruct Granny's life and family history through the stories they tell. What they recall of Granny's life reveals she was outspoken, spunky, wise, and independent. She had her own ideas about what right living is, but she also understood humankind's propensity for wrong-headed destructive choices in life. It is Granny who once saved Maurine from censure and self-loathing when her involvement with Howard led to her mistaken notion that she was pregnant. After nearly causing her own death by drinking tea made from cotton roots, a folk remedy she had once heard her grandmother describe, Maurine is chastised by Granny: "Maurine, you haven't got the sense of a bat. . . . There wasn't a chance in a thousand you'd do a thing but kill yourself with that mess you fixed" (58). Granny sends Maurine off to the a doctor, who confirms Granny's belief that her granddaughter was never pregnant in the first place.

When Maurine tells Granny later that she will never trust a man, Granny sets her straight once again: "Don't take too much on yourself, Maurine. . . . Be glad of living, and leave some things to the Lord. For what is to be will be" (59). Despite memories of Granny's disapproval, now that Maurine has seen Howard once again, the old distrust returns; but she admits she is still attracted to him.

Howard, however, finds Linda Kay fair game for his next amorous adventure. Bobby Joe spends days and most nights out hunting and carousing with his young male cousins, leaving his bride to spend her evenings listening to the older relatives tell stories. Howard's ardent pursuit of Linda Kay almost leads to his success and her downfall. Maurine recognizes that Linda Kay is vulnerable, and she takes on the thankless job of foiling Howard's plans. On the Fourth of July, Maurine invites Howard, Linda Kay and Bobby Joe, Howard's young daughter Debora, and her cousin Cherita to drive in for the celebration in town.

It is a gala occasion until Howard forgets who he is with while watching the beauty contestants parade. First he whispers, "God, . . . look at her swing her stuff," and then he really surrenders to lust: "Hot damn, . . . Look at them tits." Maurine reminds him where he is; and in his embarrassment, he rushes to his car. Then Bobby Joe refuses to take Linda Kay with him to purchase bootleg whiskey before the dance. Feeling rejected, Linda Kay joins Howard. The confused teenager's seduction is imminent. Maurine makes sure the event does not take place when she abruptly interrupts Howard's advances. Debora, witnessing Maurine's interference, decides she hates Maurine.

Debora has built a romantic dream around the possibility that Linda Kay and Howard will someday be a couple. Divided in her loyalty to her divorced parents, she fantasizes that Linda Kay can fill the place of her absent mother. She discusses her fantasy in her diary in the flowery language of a sentimental adolescent:

> It is a wonderful thing to watch love blossoming as if in
> the desert. How I hated this place at first. I still hate the
> hot dry winds that nearly suck the life out of you, the
> horrible dust that gets in your throat. It is already begin-
> ning to be hot here in my secret place, and I can hear the
> horrible sounds like monstrous machines of the dry-

weather bugs in the Chinese elm trees. . . .I think they are
really cicadas. . . .They say if it rains it will settle the dust
and the bugs will hush. I do not know, but it is like a
desert now, and love is blossoming like a miracle. (105)

Then confused by all that is happening around her and to her per-
sonally with the onset of her menses, Debora discovers that Maurine,
not Linda Kay, knows how to listen and to comfort. Howard loves his
daughter, but he is so absorbed in his pursuit of Bobby Joe's pretty
wife that he pays scant attention to his daughter's needs. Before she
goes to Maurine, Debora slips alone into Granny's room. As she
strokes Granny's hand she imagines she feels "the last waves of life
flowing out of Granny." She thinks "that life was a thing that belonged
to everyone for awhile, and now Granny was almost finished with it"
(164). Somehow in her sensitive adolescent soul, Debora makes connections between Granny's death to come and her own mortality.
Later she shares this experience with Maurine, expressing vaguely that
some change other than the physical has taken place in her life. Maurine understands and says:

I think maybe I see how Granny helped. I think she made
you understand, some way, that there are things that happen to us in life—natural things, that come whenever it's
time for them, and so we accept them. We go on living—
or, if that's what it's time for, we die. (167)

The emotional entanglements of Granny's granddaughters are not
the only conflicts plaguing the family. Maurine's church-going sister
Juanita worries that there is no evidence Granny ever belonged to the
church. Granny Albright has been independent in her actions and a
free thinker religiously, although she has always insisted on right living. So far as Brother Fulkington and his New Hope Church members are concerned, to join this church, identified by Rushing in con-

versation as the Church of Christ, the prospective member must be baptized by immersion. Juanita tells Maurine that the preacher will be compelled to reveal this fact to the congregation at Granny's funeral. Troubled, family members remember vaguely that Granny probably joined the Primitive Baptists, more often called the Hardshell Baptists, whose guiding philosophy was Granny's belief that "what is to be, will be." Juanita wants proof. If Granny is not a member of her church, "the one true Church," then for Juanita cloudy surmises are not enough.

Maurine, who knows what a great and forgiving spirit Granny possessed becomes impatient with Juanita's concern with what people may think at Granny's funeral; but because she cares about her sister's feelings, she reluctantly goes with Juanita to discover what Brother Fulkington may know about Granny's spiritual life. The good preacher is uncertain. Finally, he says, "Girls, I think I was always just a little afraid of your granny, for the time when I was about ten years old and she took a peach-tree limb to me for getting into her cake-box." Then he adds sheepishly, "May the good Lord forgive me, but I never had the nerve to ask her if she was saved" (117–18). For Maurine, that admission ends the discussion: "Then it looks like . . . that it's going to stay between Granny and the Lord" (117–18).

Granny had always said that when her time came, she was ready to go. When Mama Albright leaves Linda Kay in charge one afternoon while she goes to town for a dental appointment, the rains come and Granny's long life quietly ends. When Linda Kay realizes Granny is gone, she finds she has the courage to bathe Granny for burial, lovingly and without flinching. Howard shows up to patronize "poor little Linda" who, he says, must be scared. She assures him she is not and sends him to spread the news of Granny's death. Linda has shown she has what it takes to be an Albright woman and Granny's successor someday.

All of the recoverable events of Granny's life are gathered here into a family saga, which strengthens tenuous individual connections and reconnects relatives who have lost track of their significance to each other. Granny has left as her heritage her commonsense understanding of human mistakes, particularly for Maurine. In the letter to Maurine to be opened after Granny's death, she bequeaths Maurine her most treasured possession, a pearl and ruby ring. She has never said who gave it to her. Maurine guesses it was a gift from a long-ago lover. In her letter, Granny's explanation is that "It was give to me in my young girlhood by somebody you never did hear tell of and that don't make no difference now" (191). With this letter, Granny leaves no other material possessions. Her legacy instead goes to granddaughter Maurine, who has known Granny best in her role as a Grandmother of West Texas. Granny, whose life has provided her well-lived days as an example, is gone. A new Albright woman takes her place. Clearly Linda Kay will someday be Granny's successor. Maurine, despite her status as a spinster, will serve well enough as the Grandmother figure while Linda Kay grows into the role.

Soon after her second novel was published, another Texan, Margaret Cousins, who had a distinguished career as a magazine and book editor in New York, became Rushing's editor for a brief while. She wrote Rushing that Fred Gipson, also a Texas native and author of the popular novel *Old Yeller*, had discussed *Against the Moon* in a letter to her. Gipson said "he had a feeling that the Albrights might be the family that lived down the road from him." Rushing took Gipson's remark as "high praise" but adds, "[W]hen the people in and around my old hometown began trying to decide just which local person each character represented [in *Against the Moon*], I couldn't feel quite so well satisfied. One of my aunts said 'That little silly one was me, wasn't she?'" In typical understatement, she adds, "I felt like saying, 'Why Auntie, I wouldn't have thought you had it in you.' But I just smiled and let her think what pleased her (*Against the Moon* ix)." Rarely does Rushing discuss local response to her often negative portrayal of West Texas natives as she does here.

As Rushing looks back at her techniques for developing the characters in this novel in the reprint introduction, she admits this story
might not be believable set in the late twentieth century:

> The events of *Against the Moon* would be unlikely to hap-
> pen now, I suppose, even in remote country places. At
> least they would not happen in quite the same way. But
> country people who live in harmony with their environ-
> ment still move with the rhythms of nature. There are still
> among them old men who can look at the sky and say
> with calm certainty that a cloud won't come up against
> the moon.

Significantly Rushing concludes, "They are the ones who understand,
because they feel it in their bones, that 'to everything there is a season,
and a time to every purpose under the heaven'" (x). In her fiction to
follow, Rushing continues to honor this deeply felt association with
nature she sees in the inhabitants of her native region.

With her first two novels, Rushing began to acquire a modest
readership. Critical response to *Walnut Grove* was somewhat noncommittal, if the *Booklist* review is typical. According to this critic, the
novel is "undistinguished but honest and satisfying in substance" (qtd.
in S. Bennett 46). When *Against the Moon* appeared four years later,
however, Rushing was assured that her five-year plan had led to success as a novelist. *Publisher's Weekly* judged the novel superior in its
portrayal of family relationships. That year, *Redbook* magazine
included a lengthy excerpt of the novel under the title "Albright
Women" in its May issue. In 1969 the novel was published by Wegner
in Hamburg, Germany as *Geh Schlaffen, mein Herz, es ist Zeit*.

❧ *Chapter 4* ❧

TEXAS MYTHS REVISED

PERHAPS MORE THAN ANY OTHER woman writer in Texas during the early 1960s, Rushing exemplifies with her first novels the transition occurring in the fiction Texas women were writing. Although it uses traditional plot development that moves forward without complication for the first two sections, *Walnut Grove* does not conclude with the expected certainty that all will turn out well for the protagonist, John Carlile, as it might have in the novels many women writers were publishing in 1964. He will leave the region, but he has no idea what to expect in the future. In *Against the Moon*, the story line might have mimicked the stories the teenage bride, Linda Kay, enjoyed reading in *True Romance* magazines. Description of the near seduction of an innocent young woman might have appeared in one of Linda Kay's favorite stories, but formulaic novels would have given Linda Kay a starring role. Instead she becomes one of three women characters working through complications in their lives through their connections with the influential past and the immediate presence of the dying grandmother.

For more than thirty years, women writers in the state had found producing formulaic short stories with happy and predictable endings for popular magazines so lucrative that most did not demonstrate much ambition for writing literary fiction, which did not always end with "they lived happily ever after." Beginning in the 1920s, Texans Katherine Anne Porter and Winifred Sanford ignored formulas and published fiction of substance, but few other women writers followed their example. Then in the early sixties, as popular periodicals began to compete with television, publication of fiction became more selective and scarce.

Many Texas women writers signed up for university creative writing classes with the desire to create more substantial short stories. The careers of Mary Gray Hughes, Pat Carr, and Carolyn Osborn as writers of quality short fiction began in this decade, but Rushing is one of the few Texas women writers who, as a well-educated English major, lifelong reader, and savvy collector of her native region's history, began to recognize the possibilities in her materials for well-made literary novels. For Rushing, production of her first two novels developed skills in both character development and creation of a plausible story line. Although the narrative in both novels is disciplined by forceful themes, Rushing had yet to demonstrate the skills that would give her next two novels psychological complexity, as well as the intellectual impact that thoughtful social criticism conveys.

For these two novels, *Tamzen* and *Mary Dove*, Rushing focuses on what life in her native region might have been before the farmers arrived. With her knowledge and understanding of the people and history of the area, Rushing is not willing to accept the themes and myths treasured by writers of genre Westerns. Whatever their sympathies, creators of Westerns most often assume the arrival of nesters somehow interfered with the rancher's admirable vision for the great spaces of the West. In *Mary Dove*, Rushing moves back in history to the earliest occupation of the Rolling Plains by cattle and sheep ranchers around the 1870s. In this novel, Rushing contradicts the treasured notion that the early cowboy was an independent wanderer, valuing freedom more than commitment. In *Tamzen* Rushing chooses a point of view counter to accepted Western myth in two significant ways. Her sympathies lie with homesteaders in the traditional conflict between ranchers who have enjoyed free range for several decades and determined nesters who aim to settle on their claims and raise families. Even more contradictory to traditional Westerns, Rushing chooses for the narrator a strong, intelligent young woman, whose determined efforts to make a home in West Texas drives the action in the novel.

For *Walnut Grove* and *Against the Moon*, Rushing depended exclusively on regional oral history and personal impressions and memories for her materials. In *Tamzen* and *Mary Dove*, the writer allows her imagination to roam freely through the possibilities suggested by adopting a new angle of vision for relating early history of the too-late frontier and depicting the people who came first to settle there.

Tamzen (1972)

Rushing, perhaps without consciously planning such boldness, became an innovator in her third novel. With her knowledge of the stories of pioneer life on the Rolling Plains came her understanding of the vital participation of women in the settlement of the West Texas frontier. What if she told that story from the woman's point of view, and in the end the homesteader triumphs over the cattleman? What if, too, the cowboy marries a determined young woman and settles down to become a farmer? Following the conventions of the traditional Western novel would in no way capture the character of the early woman settler as Rushing knew her through the tales her maternal grandmother had told her. Western myth had ignored the stalwart woman pioneer as a major figure in the settlement of the West. Turning the myth upside down, Rushing created Tamzen Greer.

Jane Rushing often implicitly comments on the role of women on the West Texas frontier in her work. In *Starting from Pyron*, she describes her mother Mabel Adams's memories of growing up in the early twentieth century with two brothers. As a nine-year-old, Mabel assisted with cooking and cleaning during the years her family owned the Pyron Hotel. Her two brothers hauled freight from a nearby town, hung around the hotel with their friends, and enjoyed watching the railroad construction workers. Rushing says, "Nearly everything

was more fun for boys than for girls, and these glory days when the
railroad came were no exception." One of their early folk songs
described the plight of the frontier girl:

> Boys don't have to milk nor churn, nor do they wish to try—
> Riding horses, driving cattle, eating cake and cherry pie.

The ditty ends with the declaration: "Ain't I glad that I'm a boy" (32).
Even on the rare occasions when Mabel accompanied her brothers
when they drove to nearby Wastella to pick up freight, her brothers
ordered her to drive as fast as she could make the mules run. The two
boys ran ahead, and as the wagon whizzed by they practiced "hanging
freights," as catching a train on the move was called, anticipating the
time when the rail line would finally reach Pyron.

For Mabel's mother, life on the too-late frontier demanded even
more of women settlers as they struggled to provide livable homes for
their families. In the brief appendix to Clyde Gilmore's "Recollections," Mabel describes her own mother's early home:

> I've heard a lot about our dirt kitchen floor at this first
> place I lived. Mama had to work hard to keep it smooth
> and clean. She would sprinkle ashes over it and sweep
> that off. Sometimes she would sprinkle salt and sweep
> that about over the floor—always working to keep it dry.
> She liked to tell about one morning she had almost fin-
> ished churning when some neighbors came in to "stay all
> day." While Mama was in the front room asking them in
> and making excuses for the house not being "cleaned up,"
> one of the boys ran through the kitchen and turned the
> churn of buttermilk over on her nice clean floor!

With stories like these, all revealing the woman's life on the early
Rolling Plains, Rushing had ample material for creating the sturdy,

resolute Tamzen. When Rushing defined her recurring character, the Grandmother of West Texas, she says that by the time she wrote *Tamzen*, she seemed to have decided, though not consciously, that she needed to eliminate the grandmother figure from subsequent novels. The writer admits then, that after all, Tamzen was modeled more closely on her Grandmother Adams than any other character in her fiction. Rushing adds, "[Tamzen] was what I thought my maternal grandmother would have been at nineteen, based on many stories she had told me of her girlhood, as well as my own mature view of her as a woman" ("The Grandmother" 39). What Tamzen's characterization turns out to be is that of a West Texas Grandmother in the making.

Rushing catalogs with precise detail the characteristics Tamzen Greer will bring to her role as a future Grandmother of West Texas:

She has already learned how to be a pioneer housewife in West Texas. She has done battle with the never-ending sandstorms and found out how to trick them by hanging out the washing early in the morning so it will dry before they strike. And she has tacked up cloth on the bare ceiling joists to catch the dirt that filters down through the crude shingled roof. She will know how to protect a new-born babe from dust-laden air by spreading a dampened cloth above its crib. She will know how to cope when the two-year-old turns over a churn full of buttermilk on the freshly swept dirt floor of the kitchen, just as company knocks at the front door. She will learn what to do about croup when the doctor is twenty miles away and a blizzard is blowing in from the north. She will see to it that her children go to school and behave themselves, that they grow up knowing right from wrong, and that they marry decent husbands and wives. ("The Grandmother" 41)

With these characteristics in mind, Rushing creates an adventur-
ous young woman open to change if it leads to a better life. When
news of the possibilities for acquiring free land in West Texas appears
in the local newspaper, Walter Greer discusses the article with
Tamzen, his oldest daughter. The prospect of homesteading in West
Texas intrigues both father and daughter. Tamzen, determined, capable, and optimistic, sees an opportunity for her widowed father when
he contemplates leaving his East Texas farm and striking out to settle
public land soon to be available. Not sure of what he will do when he
arrives on the frontier, Walter has no large vision, feeling only a need
to leave his farm for a new environment after his wife's death. On the
other hand, Tamzen, the caretaker daughter of the motherless family,
has qualms about leaving her comfortable existence, but she possesses
an innate ability to be at home anywhere. Her younger sister, Lutie, is
less certain about the move.

For Tamzen, leaving her tidy home and the comfort of being near
her mother's grave makes the possibility of selling out difficult to face.
After a ray of sunlight focuses on her mother's tombstone as Tamzen
wrestles with her reluctance to leave, this young woman who believes
in signs decides that "[i]t was like a picture of God's grace coming
down through stormy heavens." For Tamzen then, this was a "place
apart, and could always be" (26). The family cemetery need not be
sold; and if that is so, she is ready to go West. Her father agrees and
negotiates with the county to supervise the family graveyard in the
future and puts the farm on the market. Walter Greer was "a man
more inclined to look forward than backward, yet not a foresighted
man either," but by the fall, Walter, Tamzen, her sister Lutie, and her
brother Dan are on their way to West Texas (29). Although Tamzen
suspects their new home may be very different from the home she
leaves, she faces her new life optimistically.

Soon after they arrive on the Rolling Plains, the Greer family
finds themselves embroiled in a range war over who has rights to the
railroad land known as Block 97—the early cattlemen or the latecom-

ing nesters. What Rushing seems to have decided as she planned to write *Tamzen* is that formulas for fiction about range wars needed reexamining. The would-be farmers become the heroes in this dispute over ownership of Block 97, which occurred in a slightly different time frame in Texas history, but involved the feuds between cattle ranchers and homesteaders developed in the novel.

In the Rushing archives in the Southwest Collection at Texas Tech University, one file preserves Rushing's extensive research into the Block 97 controversy history of the region before she wrote a six-page summary of her "Plans for a Novel About Block 97." In a lengthy manuscript intended for submission to the Snyder branch of the Ranch Headquarters Association, Rushing discusses how the squabbles over West Texas railroad land became almost mythical in the folklore of the region. She adds, "These stories, like many myths of all ages, had their basis in fact—heart-breaking, real-life experiences all across the West." Rushing admits she probably never uncovered the factual story completely. She adds, however, that "the legendary aspect of the story enhances its interest and emphasizes its significance" (4).

In her research, Rushing discovered that the land designated as Block 97 had been granted to the Houston and Texas Central Railroad in the 1870s to provide right-of-way for the highly desired rail line. Meanwhile, the legislature, out of ignorance of the Houston and Texas Central claim or their intrigue with the notion that Jay Gould planned to run the Texas and Pacific across West Texas, granted a generous reservation for that line. Cattle ranchers ran their cattle with little charge on the West Texas railroad lands until the state discovered that what they chose to call their clerical error had left ownership uncertain. To settle the controversy, the state finally declared the land public domain in 1899 and announced that Block 97 would soon be open to claims by homesteaders. In a prefatory note to *Tamzen*, Rushing explains she has compressed history because the legal settlement of the historical dispute took place later than described in her novel, set in the 1890s.

When Tamzen arrives with her family to settle on a claim on these now public lands, she discovers, as did Rushing's Grandmother Adams, that her new home will be an unpainted, two-room box-and-strip house. The dirt-floored lean-to on the back serves as kitchen. No ceilings protect the rooms from constant sifting dust; and their furniture includes only feather mattresses, two cane-bottomed chairs, a table, and a lamp. Isolated on the Rolling Plains prairies in this meager environment, Tamzen, Lutie, and Dan soon recognize that their life there will include struggling with water shortage and coping with dust storms. Before long they learn that not the least of their problems are defiant cowboys bent on driving the nesters off their grasslands.

Those readers with knowledge of Dorothy Scarborough's once infamous novel *The Wind* (1925) will recognize in Tamzen and Lutie many of the characteristics Scarborough contrasts in her portrayals of Cora, a hardy ranch wife, and Letty, a frail Southern belle unable to cope with the isolation and loneliness she encounters after coming West from Virginia and marrying a cowboy. Tamzen, not yet a wife, resembles Cora in her determination to make the homesteader's life her future, although she has more understanding of Lutie's disillusionment and homesickness than Cora, who seems unaware of Letty's distress. Nevertheless, the contrast between Tamzen's approach to life and that of Lutie, her younger sister, serves to emphasize Tamzen's ability to make a home wherever she is.

One cold, lonely evening, Lutie begs Tamzen to persuade their father to go back home. The rancher Turk Bascom's cowboys have driven them away from the windmill providing water, burned their cowshed, and assured the nesters they will shoot trespassers on Bascom's range land. Such hardships convince Tamzen that she must provide for her family's protection from such threats. Adversity only makes her more resolute. When Lutie begins begging to return to East Texas, Tamzen scolds her. "Hush," she says. "We didn't come to go back" (123). Tamzen, the determined Grandmother of West Texas in the making, sees promise in the future here; and she aims to make her permanent home on the Rolling Plains. She soon proves she can hold her own with those determined that the family should leave.

Countering the unpleasantness of Turk Bascom's efforts to drive the Greers off his free range, Arthur Field, one of his cowboys, becomes a regular welcomed visitor in the Greer home. Englishmen often appear in Western fiction as cattlemen owning vast acres or as trophy hunters taking advantage of Western hospitality. Here again, Rushing refuses to be influenced by stereotypes. Arthur Field is from England, but he is not likely ever to be a big-time rancher, nor did he ever hunt big game for sport. Arthur is only a cowboy and that from necessity. His story in no way exemplifies the romance of the mythical cowboy's life. An orphan, Arthur left England when he was eighteen. His search for his main chance has led him to the Rolling Plains. What he finds is that for a time his buffalo hunting will furnish a living, but before long the buffaloes have been harvested too diligently, and that means of survival disappears. Arthur takes a job as a hand on Turk Bascom's LeGrande Ranch. He dreams of establishing his own ranch on land he hopes to homestead, but a long drouth and the Block 97 legal wrangles have killed that dream. All he owns is a dugout lined with the books he has brought to Texas, uncertain claim to a small ranch, and a few scrawny cows suffering from the prolonged dry weather plaguing the area.

Arthur joins Tamzen, Lutie, and brother Dan in evening reading sessions after they become comfortable with one another. Although it is doubtful he identifies with the hero of *Idylls of the King*, which he reads to his friends, Arthur stands by his principles as steadfastly as the legendary King Arthur. Interestingly, too, Arthur yearns to write an epic about the West. His main problem: he has found no hero worthy of such grand treatment.

The traditional struggle between the rancher Turk Bascom and Walter Greer, considered to be a "squatter" on the cowman's land, begins almost the day the Greers arrive, but Tamzen proves to be Turk's fiercest adversary. Rushing departs once again from the for-

mula in her descriptions of the conflict. Although the nesters organize
to fight back when Bascom's cowboys begin to wreck property and
threaten those seeking water at ranch windmills, their encounters are
more scare tactics on the rancher's part and bluffing retaliation by the
settlers. Little property damage occurs, and no one gets shot. Tragedy
results, nevertheless. Ironically, it is Lutie who falls victim in this still
nearly lawless land. When the nesters gather in the settlement to celebrate the news from Austin that the railroad land has been declared
public domain open to homesteading, Turk's cowboys, led by his reck-
less nephew Cato, race their horses through the crowd of celebrating
homesteaders, firing their pistols at the sky. One bullet goes astray and
strikes Lutie, and several days later she becomes the only casualty of
the cowboys' mindless ride.

After Lutie's death, the novel becomes Tamzen's story exclusively.
It is not Walter Greer who swears Turk Bascom must die. It is Tamzen
who believes that Turk encouraged the cowboys' rampage, and she
vows she will avenge her sister's death. Although Turk Bascom has
openly declared that he wants to marry Tamzen, and she is mightily
attracted to him physically, Tamzen has no desire to become a
rancher's wife. Her idea of right living is not that of the rancher's, she
believes. In her last confrontation with Turk, she tells him, "Whatever
else there is against us marrying, there's one main thing: you just ain't
our kind of people. The kind of life I've lived ain't the kind of life you
have in that ranch house, and I couldn't change, and you wouldn't"
(303). Always honest, even with herself, Tamzen compares Arthur
Field, gentle and warm, to the persuasive Turk; and Arthur's steadiness
comforts her as she rationalizes her decision. The settlement's lawmen
are not yet strong enough to cross Turk, who has ruled the territory
for years, and they hide their inaction behind an excuse that they can
not prove which cowboy's bullet brought Lutie down. Tamzen has no
fear; she believes that Turk is behind the rampage, and the murderer
must be punished.

As Rushing has described the Grandmother of West Texas, one of this prototype's most unshakable traits is her "iron-bound Puritan morality, which formed the foundation of her being" ("The Grandmother" 39). That personality quality fuels what for Tamzen is a righteous obsession, and she proves she possesses the grit to demand Old Testament justice applied to her sister's murderer, whoever he is. Arthur, who has been uncertain which Greer sister he wanted as a wife, was first attracted to Lutie, whose prettiness and compliant good nature seemed to be traits he would like in a future partner. Tamzen has seen that Arthur has always preferred Lutie's company, so according to her moral code, it is Arthur's duty to avenge Lutie's death and go after Turk. Arthur tries to reason with the implacable young woman. She reminds Arthur, "There's been a killing done . . . and no denying that. And I can tell you one thing; if I was a man, and a girl had been killed that meant anything to me, I wouldn't rest till her killer was punished. The Bible says a eye for a eye and a tooth for a tooth: if men haven't got any laws to punish the wicked, God has" (263).

Dan, always an admirer of Arthur, comes to his defense by reminding his sister that the Bible also mentions turning the other cheek. Tamzen has an answer for that: "Jesus Christ didn't come to change a jot or a tittle of the law" (263). She sends Arthur away when he tries to persuade her of the folly of her request. As expected, Tamzen's irrational desire for revenge leads to another tragedy. Dan finally shoots Turk's careless nephew Cato, who had led the cowboys' exuberant interruption of the celebration, but only after Cato accuses Dan of stealing Bascom cattle. As in much of Rushing's fiction, tragedy always follows moral lapses when individuals or communities are guided by inflexible religious beliefs.

Tamzen's rejection of Arthur's company causes her great pain. When he comes to report Cato's death, Tamzen makes clear that nothing's changed unless he is the one who killed the irresponsible young cowboy. He assures her he is not the killer. Tamzen, irrational in her desire for punishment of her sister's killer and uncertain about

Arthur's feelings toward her, begins to dream muddled dreams and "look peaked." As she stands in front of a mirror, this twenty-one-year-old nester decides she looks thirty years old and is losing her looks, her health, and "maybe her mind." Her conclusion: "You've got a life to live, and you've got to live it like God intended; .you've got to take hold of yourself" (265). Resolve leads to reassessment, and Tamzen soon resumes her energetic care of her father and her brother.

When the Block 97 controversy is finally legally settled in favor of the nesters, Arthur has to decide whether he will join Turk in his trek to Wyoming. Tamzen has her own dilemma. Turk wants to take her with him too. She refuses, but somehow she feels compelled to understand how she could be so strongly attracted to two men. She rationalizes:

> Well, a woman could love two men. Or love one and lust
> after another. Or else why did the Bible tell so many
> times what must be done to an adulteress?. . . Surely
> women must have been tempted through all the cen-
> turies, but must often have resisted temptation, for there
> was praise of virtuous women, with price beyond rubies.
> (304)

Finally, lonesome and still uncertain, she squelches her pride and goes to Arthur's dugout, and together they decide to stay on what will now be her land because her father and brother are striking out once again to an as yet unknown destination. An old squatter, it turns out, has witnessed Cato's shooting and threatens to turn Dan in if he is not paid to stay quiet. As the reconciled Tamzen and Arthur make plans for their future, Arthur tentatively points out one of the problems for him as a cowboy turning farmer. "Tamzen," he says, "I don't even know how to plow." Tamzen is a pragmatist. She reassures her future

husband: "Arthur, . . . I can teach you" (313). Arthur already knows
Tamzen's strengths. He has just listened to her sensible plans for the
future:

> He could sell his improvements to some new settler, and
> they could use the money to complete the work Walter
> had started. Put up a windmill, build a floor in the
> kitchen, maybe weatherboard the house and paint it.
> Build a yard fence, have a garden and flowers—her color
> rose and her eyes sparkled as she visualized the future and
> forgot for the moment both the past and the present.
> (312)

Then Arthur admits willingly that life with Tamzen is his future.

The myth dictates that Arthur, an independent cowboy soon to
become a nester to fit a woman's idea of what life should be on these
plains, will never be content as a farmer. Rushing, in one of the most
cogent observations in the novel, draws the distinction between the
rancher's vision for these grasslands and the farmer's intentions when
he views his prairie acres. As Arthur considers his choices, he decides
the farmer is "a different breed from the ranchers who had come to
take the land for kingdoms, or the cowboys who worked and fought
for them, with a loyalty that often matched that of knights in the old
stories." He continues with the observation that this tie between
rancher and cowboy and between the cowmen themselves "gave rise
to the ranchers' belief that they had a monopoly on honor. A rancher's
word was as good as his bond, any cowman would tell you, and this
was often true, no matter whose land he grazed or whose cattle he
branded" (230).

On the other hand, Arthur knows that the "nester wanted no
kingdom, neither did he want a king." Arthur has observed that farmers will go out of their way to help a neighbor, but "the farmer's ideal

was to be his own man, beholden to no one, with no one beholden to him." Arthur concludes this reverie that leads finally to his decision to become a farmer:

> This was the farmer's ideal. Like the rancher, who lauded
> honor among his peers while he knew they were stealing
> his cattle, he was somewhat blinded to reality. The farmer
> might be free of entanglements with other men, but
> Arthur guessed he could never do without a woman. For
> one thing, it was hard to imagine a settler without a fam-
> ily—to see what other motivation he could have for
> building a snug house, raising crops that just made a liv-
> ing, organizing a church, supporting a school. The settlers'
> ways were guided by women, and much of his success
> was due to the work of women. (230)

Arthur then admits to himself that life as a farmer offers none of the footloose freedom he has known; he will be sharing with this woman the responsibilities required of a farmer and family man. To convince himself this choice is the best for him, he decides "he was only turn-ing back to meet civilization. So far in the world, that had always meant families and the influence of women; it had not seemed, on the whole, such a bad thing" (231).

In her creation of Arthur Field, Rushing deliberately rejects the stereotypical concept that the cowpuncher enjoys life as an independ-ent, wandering man on horseback. Instead Rushing makes clear that Arthur's decision to become a farmer is the trade-off few fictional cowboys would have considered. Hewey Callaway, Elmer Kelton's stubbornly resistant cowboy in *The Good Old Boys*, holds out until the reality of aging catches up with him. Hewey reluctantly settles down with the patient schoolteacher, Spring, in *The Smiling Country*, sequel to *The Good Old Boys*; but fictional cowboys usually end up as stove-up wanderers or more often become cattle barons if their luck prevails. Arthur may someday remember with nostalgic regret his buffalo hunting adventures and his cowpoke experiences riding for Turk Bascom, who in stories no doubt will have attained legendary stature, but he will be telling those stories to entertain his and Tamzen's children and grandchildren. Predictably Tamzen has the last word about the subject. As the newlyweds come back to Tamzen's homestead, they foresee the final settlement of the nester-rancher dispute. Arthur says, "Now I believe it really is the end." to which Tamzen answers, "No, Arthur, it's the beginning" (318).

Although Rushing does not discuss the obvious goals she seemed to keep in mind as she wrote this novel, in this exploration of a West Texas land dispute between cattlemen and nesters, the formula for genre Westerns applies not at all in Rushing's imagined frontier. Not only does she choose the nester's point of view with a woman as hero, but she also abandons the formula completely when the rancher, not the nester, loses the battle for the disputed land and his most competent cowboy turns nester. Tamzen, the author says, "knew what she wanted: a good living, a righteous life, all the old ways she knew and believed in, transported to a strange new land. With Arthur she thought she could have all this" ("The Grandmother" 40). Her creator adds that "Tamzen as Arthur knows her is not quite the total Pioneer Woman, but there is little doubt that she will be." Tamzen "does not yet (like the famous Madonna of the Trail) carry a babe in her arms while a toddler tugs at her skirts, but surely she will soon fit that image. . . . Inevitably, inexorably, Tamzen will become the Grandmother of West Texas" ("The Grandmother" 40–41).

Near the conclusion of the novel, when Arthur tells Turk he has no intention of following him further west, Turk reluctantly accepts Arthur's decision and says, "Well, you can read more books. And maybe write that poem, whatever it was, you used to talk about." Arthur says he doubts he will write the epic now. He adds, "For one thing, I never found a hero. Unless, after all, it turns out to be Tamzen" (314). This novel does not presume to be epic in intent, but Rushing fulfills her aim to portray an indomitable woman protagonist capable of heroic response to the difficulties facing the women settlers on the Rolling Plains.

A review of *Tamzen* in the *Library Journal,* praising the "sense of authenticity" in the novel, observes that Rushing's skills continue to improve and predicts this novel will become a classic in Southwestern American literature (qtd. in S. Bennett 48). Realistic portrayal of a region depends on an author's insight into the nature of its people. If Tamzen's characterization invites description as authentic, Rushing accomplishes that realism with her ability to convey a sincere concept of Western pioneer women as "moving forces."

Mary Dove (1974)

Rushing created Tamzen from the images family storytellers projected on her receptive imagination as well as from her own perceptions of the pioneer woman's strengths. Unlike Tamzen, however, Mary Dove seems to have appeared fully developed demanding her story be told. Racism is not a subject much associated with the homogeneous society of the too-late frontier. Nevertheless, Rushing grew up with the sure knowledge that, along with anti-intellectualism and xenophobia, prejudice against African Americans warped attitudes and affected emotions of the early frontier settlers, many of Southern origin, including those with whom she had been most connected as she grew up. With this fourth novel, she confronts prejudice against blacks as it existed on the West Texas frontier even more boldly than she did in *Walnut Grove.*

In the discussion of her conception of *Mary Dove* in "The Roots of a Novel," the writer admits she has no idea where Mary Dove, this mulatto girl brought up in an isolated cave in the Breaks, originated. "All I know is that suddenly I was aware of her inside me, struggling to get out" (10). In 1972 Rushing returned alone to Camp Springs in the Breaks when she began researching an article on the region, which subsequently appeared in *Early Ranching and Water Resources in*

West Texas. The settlement, now almost a ghost town, sprang up about 1880 and thrived for several decades beside a spring-fed pond, which was known as the Baptizin' Hole. Without a conscious plan, when she revisited the Baptizin' Hole and its surroundings, Rushing says the idea for the novel literally seized her imagination. What followed she describes as a "catalytic experience." With no thought at the time of choosing this particular region as the setting for a novel, she continued after her visit to return in her imagination to this isolated ranch land. Then while viewing the television version of Thomas Hardy's novel, *Far from the Madding Crowd*, the pastoral setting of the drama appealed to her imagination. Rushing writes that she "seemed to become disassociated from Hardy's characters and plot and instead began to set into motion in [her] mind a force that never stopped until [she] had written . . . *Mary Dove*" (10). Rushing explains this sudden, gripping inspiration in her history of how the novel came to be written, but why and how her writer's imagination began to create a story she did not expect remains a mystery to her.

Nevertheless, Rushing understands the transformation of the idea into a novel plot. From her experience, Rushing shares this advice:

> If there was anything different about the writing of *Mary Dove*, I think it was the intensity with which I did just about what I had been doing all along. If there is anything at all in the experience that could be illuminating to new writers, . . . I think it is the effect that an absorbing interest—a deep and abiding concern—may have upon the work of a writer who submits to it. ("Roots" 10).

Rushing understands her process of writing so well that she is able to trace clearly the evolution of both character and plot, once the protagonist appears:

> I barely spoke to anyone. I spent the day scribbling words,

phrases, fragments—later practically undecipherable—in
soft lead pencil on ruled paper salvaged by my husband
from students' examination books. (It occurs to me that
all my characters for all my books seem to have come
into being through the medium of blue-book pages and
soft lead pencils. I hardly refer to the notes later. They
aren't for reference, anyway; that is just the way the characters have of getting into my mind).

She concludes, "At the end of the day, the girl had emerged. The
spring had begun to flow, the pool filled, and Mary Dove stood beside
it" ("Roots" 10).

More spontaneous in creation than any of her other novels, *Mary
Dove* develops Rushing's obvious desire to retell the Adam and Eve
story, echoing as well the themes of Milton's epic, *Paradise Lost*. She
says she "deliberately made parallels with Milton" and wanted to
name the novel "Their Solitary Way," a quote from *Paradise Lost*, but
Doubleday did not find the title "catchy" enough. Rushing admits
also that the idea of isolating a young girl in a beautiful but lonely section of rough country was "distinctly a romantic concept (belonging
to the Romantic period, that is) and not one to be accepted by every
modern reader." She adds:

> This I knew. But tempted, myself, to believe in the sim-
> plicity and beauty of a life uncorrupted by "man's inhu-
> manity to man," I decided to attempt a plot in which this
> possibility would be explored. . . . I do not offer *Mary
> Dove* as an example of the technically perfect novel. But I
> feel that any success it has with a reader can be attributed
> to my basic feeling for the land, and my concept of a
> young girl growing up close to that land and so depend-
> ent upon it that she becomes almost an embodiment of
> its spirit ("Roots" 11).

After Rushing spent a day immersed in her notes, *Mary Dove* took shape, faster than any other of her novels. In some ways, what emerged, according to the author, is a fantasy. With Milton's epic as her inspiration, Rushing soon recognized that she wanted her plot to develop "the simple joy of a relationship between mankind and uncorrupted nature, the necessity for companionship and love, and . . . the development of a society that introduces a new element: sin, but not without hope" ("Roots" 46).

Mary Dove opens with a traditional description of the lone rider on the open range:

> In the time of a strange withered spring, a lone cowboy
> rode through the country where scattered little flat-
> topped hills rose sharply above a rolling terrain watered
> by narrow running streams. He stayed, when he could, on
> the high places, so nothing got between him and the
> great clean sky and he could look across the desolate
> browned land to rest his eyes on the purple horizon. (1)

Christopher Columbus "Red" Jones, riding alone across the Breaks of the Rolling Plains in the early 1880s, seems at first to be no less than the re-creation of Rushing's version of the mythical cowboy, perhaps more aware of nature than most, but free and unhampered in his actions. But Red Jones is not just a cowpoke. He is a feeling, troubled young man who longs for connections with others in his isolated job as a cowboy on the Bar Diamond Ranch. On this spring day, idyllic as it may seem, Red is riding toward a tragic scene that will reveal the cowboy's empathy for those like him, isolated from society. He finds the body of a man he knows only as Pardue, who has followed his sheep herd over a steep bluff in a late-winter blizzard. Although Red hardly knew Pardue, a tight-lipped sheep man trying to survive in cattle country, he knows he must bury him. It troubles Red that he may be the only one to ever know where the reclusive sheep herder is buried. He knows no words to make this a proper burial except "God help you, Pardue." Not convinced that is enough, he calls as he rides away, "Goodbye, old hoss" (4).

When Pardue did not return from his search for his sheep during the unexpected blizzard, his daughter Mary Dove searches the Breaks around her cavelike dugout home for signs of her father. Finally she finds the rotting carcasses of the sheep and sadly assumes her father's body is buried beneath them. Isolated from society by a father who knows her mixed blood will perpetuate a harsher isolation once their primitive home is discovered, Mary Dove has grown up without human companionship other than that of Pardue. After she accepts that she has been orphaned by the capriciousness of West Texas weather, Mary Dove survives alone in the dugout, which is located near a spring. Her companions are her seven pet lambs, a milk cow, and the wild things around her. She finds in her loneliness some comfort in her feeling that a strong spiritual presence resides in the natural world around her, although her father, in his untutored way, has shared with her only a limited knowledge of God. Nevertheless, Mary's strong sense of the presence of God sustains her and reassures her in the loss of her father, even though he had never been able to explain the concept of a creator to her. In her effort to understand both the coming and going of the seasons and her father's death, Mary Dove reasons:

> She guessed spring and earth went on forever, made out
> of lives God took to renew them, to renew them con-
> stantly as people kept putting fuel on a fire when they ran
> out of matches. Maybe God had no matches . . . and if the
> fire ever went out spring and earth would end, the world
> would end. She guessed it never would end though,
> because life went on renewing life—going back to the
> earth, coming out of the earth, forever and ever. Because

God was not a sheepherder in a dugout far from town,
using up his matches. God was the fuel and the fire and
the fire builder too. (21)

Mary Dove decides with her usual unaffected wisdom that "God
must be so far from being like people that the kind of talk people used
couldn't say anywhere near what God was" (24). She will soon learn
that this simple assessment of traditional religious beliefs may explain
why church people behave so differently than she had expected.

In many ways, Mary Dove is a pantheist, who in her isolation finds
kinship with the spiritual in her natural surroundings. In her essay on
this novel's creation, Rushing says, "Mary Dove . . . is understandable
only in terms of the special way in which she viewed the world
around her, and it therefore became essential that nature (in the
Romantic sense) should be a factor and that detailed descriptions of
the setting be given in order to present her pantheism" ("Roots" 11).
The author's own love for her native land, her knowledge of nine-
teenth-century Romantics' works and theories, and her consequent
philosophy of life are clearly catalysts in her creation of this novel.

Rushing does not stray from the Romantic concept of the nature
of society, in which, once the innocent girl must confront people, she
experiences prejudice, though she never fully understands how
destructive unfounded hatred can be. The author identifies this West
Texas brand of "inhumanity to man" when she says their unrecog-
nized cruelty "grows out of a characteristic brand of frontier Protestantism, in which Christianity does not fully prevail, an attitude totally
believable to anyone familiar with this period of southwestern history" ("Roots" 46).

For a while after Mary Dove accepts that her father has died with
his flock, the lonely girl finds solace in caring for her animals, but it is
inevitable that she will soon experience unreasoning prejudice. Mary
Dove has been admonished by her father never to let a man come
near her, so when the curious Red finally finds her camp, she shoots

him out of fear. Out of compassion, she then nurses him back to
health. Puzzled at her innocence, Red is intrigued by this guileless
and attractive young woman, who says what she thinks and who,
despite her uninhibited and straightforward demeanor, possesses a
strong moral code all her own.

As Red recuperates from his bullet wound and the time
approaches when Mary Dove's innocent view of humanity will be
altered, Mary insists he explain who God is. Red describes church
where "people gets dressed up in their best clothes, and they go to the
church house, and they sing and pray and the preacher preaches to
them about the laws of God" (86). For Mary Dove, the custom of
gathering in a church house to find God is inconceivable. She feels
God's presence down at her bathing pool or when she stands on a hill
feeling the sky and clouds around her. She says to Red, "It seems like
I'm knowing just how it is to be touched by God and feeling God
myself and knowing God is everything" (87). Red finally admits he
does not know much about God.

Despite Red's ignorance of the God he grew up worshiping in a
church house, his moral precepts reflect his Southern upbringing. He
is aware that soon, if he remains in her presence, this ingenuous young
woman will become his lover. He becomes adamant that if they live
together, their relationship will need the sanction of a marriage cere-
mony. When his longing for Mary Dove physically becomes unbearable, he leaves her dugout, where he has spent several months recov-
ering from his leg wound. Upon his return late one evening he
suddenly recognizes Mary Dove's racial heritage. He experiences
great pain when he sees her "in the yellow light with her hair like a
mass of glinting wire and her breasts shining brown as her sun-loving
face as she stood revealed to him" (105). She is black. Overwhelmed
by enormous pain and confusion, Red soon leaves Mary Dove again,
believing he will return only briefly in the future to check on her
welfare. But Red loves Mary Dove.

When he returns, he feels compelled to explain to her what he

believes is her origin, as far as he can know. Earlier at Mary's suggestion, he picked the lock on a trunk belonging to Mary Dove's
mother. Never before opened by Mary Dove, the trunk provides
dresses to replace the threadbare outgrown rags Mary has been wearing. Among the everyday gingham dresses is one other dress, a fancy
costume, low-cut in front, which intrigues Mary. Red, aware of what
such a dress probably signifies, hastily calls it a party dress. Although he
does not tell Mary he suspects her mother was a dance-hall girl, or
more likely a prostitute, he is wise enough in the ways of the world to
understand the reason for Mary's biracialism.

Just before Christmas, after a lengthy absence, Red returns, knowing he must try to explain the meaning of miscegenation. He declares
they cannot marry because a law prohibits whites from marrying
blacks. Mary is puzzled. Her father was white, she says. Then Red has
to explain that the law declares that any black blood at all makes her a
mixed blood. Not God's law, he affirms as Mary puzzles over his
explanation, but state law forbids their marriage. He adds, however,
that God's law makes their mating a sin. Mary, as usual, wants to know
where in the Bible he can find such a command. Sheepishly, Red
admits he does not know, but the law can be found there because
preachers say it is, and "that's what preachers is for—to tell you what
it says" (114).

Mary Dove finally persuades Red that if society does not approve
of their love, certainly God will. Even though in his mind she is only
a half-black bastard, he finally knows "he must have her or die, and
because this way she could feel like a wife and he would have a
chance to make her happy. In the end, of course, they would go to
hell" (117). She takes him to a hilltop after their Christmas meal where
he experiences with her a spectacular West Texas sunset. As the sun
disappears in fiery red clouds, Mary Dove quietly says, "I have always
been by myself before. . . . Will it come for two?" (118). For Mary
Dove, God is manifest in this natural wonder, and both are convinced
of his presence as she sings, quietly, of "ten thousand charms," lines

from a hymn Red taught her. When in the darkening western sky a single star appears dramatically, Mary Dove and Red solemnly ritual-ize their union with promises of devotion and fidelity to each other. As they turn, Red hopes the star is the Christmas star and adds "I hope it is a blessing." Mary Dove assures him, "It's a blessing" (118–19). Their week together afterward is idyllic. They often return "to where they had made their two beds into one and cast themselves upon it, doing once again the thing that through the days and nights of their week together had brought them both delight. . . . ('What do they call it, Red?' 'I don't know of no name for it that a man can say to a decent woman')" (122).

Still torn between his love for Mary, which he believes is a sin, and his convictions, Red stays away from his lover as much as he can. Set-tlers, as is inevitable, have begun to move onto the farmland west of the Divide. Red attends the itinerant Brother Michael's camp meeting services in the new settlement near his cow camp, which he now shares with Jack Ryan, another Bar Diamond cowboy. Brother Michael, like Mary Dove, feels God's presence in these great open spaces he is experiencing for the first time, but his God demands pub-lic repentance for what he deems to be sin. Red stumbles forward asking forgiveness at the end of one emotional church service, but he cannot publicly confess what he believes his sin is—loving Mary. For Red, "the threat of hell was as real as flames in a fireplace, and the rea-son for staying out of the fire was sensible and clear" (188); but he still feels like a fool as he rides hastily away from the meeting, prayers for his salvation still echoing in his ears.

Red fears his cowboy companion Jack will eventually guess his secret. Furthermore in his effort at dissimulation, he has given Lizzie Munden, one of the settlers' daughters, the impression he is courting her. As he rides miserably toward his camp, fully aware he will have to set Lizzie straight about his intentions, he agonizes aloud, "Oh God, why did you let me do that?" He has no idea what *that* is. He didn't know which he regretted most—"his unchristian wedding with

Mary Dove, his misunderstood friendship with Lizzie, or the fool he had made of himself at the meeting" (185). His self-flagellation is cut short by the appearance of Mary Dove at his camp. Angrily Red reminds her that she was never to come near his camp. He knows, too, he must tell Mary Dove their love is doomed. To his consternation, it is Mary who insists they must part forever. Mary has come to tell him a lie, as she thinks of it. She has seen Red's lack of enthusiasm when she announces she is pregnant, and she has sensed his reluctance to share his thoughts with her anymore. She has come to the realization that their relationship is more burden than joy for Red. To ease his obvious conflicts with his conscience, Mary assures him that she no longer needs him and he need not feel responsible for her welfare. Agonizing both over what will happen to Mary and their unborn child and over his own burdensome guilt, Red leaves Mary when she insists they can no longer live together.

With a searing sense of what he assumes is his wrongdoing, Red capitulates at the next night's services and agrees to baptism, which the preacher says will wash away his sins. Red is unaware that in his long walks Brother Michael has discovered Mary's bathing pool, where she communes regularly with a nesting dove. After spending a lonely night wandering and agonizing in the moonlight, Mary finally accepts that Red will no longer be a part of her lonely life. "Mourn for me, dove," she begs as she approaches the bird's nest. As she sits on the side of the pool, she composes a song, reminiscent of a biblical Psalm:

> Mourn for me.
> You dove mourn for everything,
> But I will not mourn.
> I will be glad, and the birds on their nests
>   will be glad, and the trees, and the sweet flowers.
> You dove can do all the mourning for us.
> And all of the rest of the world

Will be glad

And find God. (196)

In her own ritualistic enactment of baptism, of washing away her sorrow, Mary undresses and plunges into the clear, cold water, where
somehow she feels comforted.

At that hour, Brother Michael leads his flock to Mary's pool to
immerse the converts in baptism. When his followers discover Mary
bathing naked in the spring, they react harshly. "I ain't gonna be baptized where no nigger's been taking a bath. . . . I'd go to hell first," one
girl yells (198). Red rescues Mary from what is becoming a mindless
mob, committing himself to a life, if not of sin, then certainly of censure: "He picked up the wet shining body in his arms and held it, kiss-
ing the mouth, calling Mary Dove back to him. It was long minutes
before he remembered that the white-clad crowd (struck still and
silent too) stood looking on" (198–99). As Mary rests in her dugout,
Red knows he does not yet have a plan for taking care of Mary, but
"he knew for sure . . . that he would keep her close to him always, and
take care of her, and beget her children. He hoped God might call
that marriage, but if it was sin then sin would be their way" (200).

Brother Michael is kind but practical and firm when he tells Red
later that they must leave the country. Mary tries once again to get a
straight answer about the nature of their sin. "Is it God's Law. . . . Or is
it people's law?" (203). Brother Michael reluctantly admits he has
never seen the answer in the Bible, but he adds, "I will say this: the
people believed you have sinned. . . . Their judgment is that they cannot tolerate your presence" (204). He advises the two to move on
westward, perhaps finding a place where they can be lawfully married
and live in peace. Nevertheless, he says they must wait to leave until
the settlers gather once again the next day at Mary's pool for the bap-
tizing, because they have insisted they want to witness the departure.
Brother Michael explains, "They want to see you go when they are
gathered together. They think it's a church thing, and will be an

example for the young people to remember" (206). Brother Michael escorts the two out of their paradise and sends them on their way, much as Milton's angel Michael leads Adam and Eve out of the Garden of Eden. Both look squarely at the congregation as they ride their horses slowly past their harsh judges. Brother Michael seems to smile at them as they leave, and Mary thinks, "He wants to think of the place we're going to, where people's laws is the same as God's" (209).

Mary Dove exemplifies the author's powerful condemnation of what the early Romantic poet Robert Burns observed is "man's inhumanity to man." Almost fifteen years before Rushing published *Mary Dove*, she had explored in vivid detail the nature of sin and humanity's "fortunate fall" from innocence in her dissertation. In her discussion in "House Symbolism in the Works of Five New England Romanticists," she places particular emphasis on the works of Nathaniel Hawthorne, concluding with an analysis of *The House of Seven Gables*. Rushing perceives that the residents of the decaying old dwelling, shut off from the world, have allowed themselves to become prisoners not in the house but in their own hearts. Rushing's concern here is with the damage that occurs when a human personality is ruled by indifference or hate and the desire for revenge. Earlier in her study, she points out that in *The Scarlet Letter* "the effects of sin upon the human heart form the main theme, yet where at the same time one is never allowed to forget that it is the iron-framed Puritan community that has brought about the situation" (103). Rushing formulates here a concept that becomes a major theme in most of her fiction: self-righteous judgment of others almost always leads to heartache and alienation for the judged. For Jane Rushing, the actions of the settlers in *Mary Dove* emphasize the darkest aspect of frontier Protestantism.

The basic religious beliefs that influenced several generations of West Texans are articulated in *Mary Dove* in the conversations and thoughts of the two lovers. Settlers on the too-late frontier differ little in their moral codes from the rigid seventeenth-century Puritans

portrayed in Hawthorne's fiction. One grew up, as Red tells Mary
Dove, going to church where the preacher would teach about God,
Jesus, and salvation. Laws of God and laws of the state might not be
the same thing, but only the preacher really knew, because he was the
one who read and understood the Bible.

When he narrates the story of Adam and Eve to Mary Dove, Red
explains he has heard the preacher say all the troubles of men and
women started in the Garden of Eden. When Mary wants to know if
it was all Eve's fault, Red admits that Eve tempted Adam to eat the
apple. He adds diplomatically, "He done it because he loved her. She
was the first to disobey God." The devil, he explains, is the opposite of
God. He rules over hell where sinners will go when they die "if they
haven't repented of their sins and joined the church and all" (188).
Repentance, baptism by immersion, and careful monitoring by
proven Christians provide the only path to salvation. When Red tells
Mary that "separating might not prove we repented, but we shore
enough couldn't go on living together and try to pretend that we was
sorry of our sin" (190), he reveals his fear not so much of God as of
community disapproval. In the end, Red's dilemma assumes the
dimensions of Huck Finn's decision to remain loyal to Jim and "go
to hell."

Rushing's conviction is that the strong beliefs and inflexible moral
code of many on this segment of the western frontier have affected
individual attitudes and community values even to the present. In all
of Rushing's fiction, this theme resonates. The writer explores lives
that have either been hemmed in by community opinion or escaped
the narrow confines of a life created by those values. Designated only
as "the church" in her novels, community judges are its members who
practice brotherhood with good-hearted caring about what happens
to their neighbors. Such solicitude can, however, degenerate into self-
righteous prying into others' affairs and sponsors a church-member
clannishness that shuts out the outsider.

Critic Becky Matthews, in her essay "Writing the Un-Western," classifies *Mary Dove* as an "un-Western." She says *Mary Dove* narrates both a love story and "an historically accurate commentary of the social mores of a particular time and place," but Matthews believes, too, that innovative structure sets the novel apart from most traditional Westerns:

> In [the novel], one finds all the elements of the stereotypical western. The traditional setting, conflict and characters are all there, but Rushing turns the formula upside down by using these elements in unexpected ways. Her approach makes this novel an "un-western" and gives new meaning to the impact of civilization on the wilderness. (65)

Chief among Rushing's departures, as Matthews explains, is the internalization of the traditional conflict between occupants of untamed land and the settler's aim to bring civilization to the wilderness. In this novel, the struggle is not between cattle barons, Indians, or outlaws and the pioneers, however. Instead, the conflict originates in Red's own conscience, where he agonizes over how to discern right from wrong. Matthews adds, "Rushing also calls into question the civilizing influence of the homesteaders" (68–69).

One reviewer called this novel "haunting," but Rushing's personal assessment of her accomplishment offers the most cogent commentary on the novel's achievement:

> I do not offer *Mary Dove* as an example of the technically perfect novel. But I feel that any success it has with a reader can be attributed to my basic feeling for the land, and my concept of a young girl growing up so close to the land and so dependent upon it that she becomes almost an embodiment of its spirit. ("Roots" 11)

Elder points out that "essentially, *Mary Dove* is a book about the simple joy of a relationship between mankind and uncorrupted nature, the necessity for companionship and love, and the development of society that in its complexity inevitably introduces the new element of sin, but not without hope. Hence, the ending of *Mary Dove* is not altogether an unhappy one" (123).

Rushing won Doubleday's LeBaron R. Barker Award for *Mary Dove*, which was published in England by Hodder and Stroughton under the title, *Shadow of the Dove*. The novel was also translated into Japanese, French, Norwegian, and Swedish. In 1990 Rushing was approached by two women film writers, eager to script *Mary Dove* and begin shopping for a producer. Halle Berry, later an Oscar winner, read the script and was enthusiastic about becoming Mary Dove in the movie. Rushing renewed the would-be film makers' option on the book for several years, but apparently no producer was willing to take the chance of making a film starring Halle Berry and a red-headed cowboy. Nevertheless, with this novel Rushing's work began to attract international attention.

Jane Rushing, almost age five, in a new sateen dress for the occasion of her
first train trip from Pyron to Hermleigh, 6.7 miles away, fall 1930.
From the Gilmore-Adams Family Collection, with permission.

This photo in the University Archives at Texas Tech was taped to a faculty
annual report dated April 11, 1956. Rushing first taught at the
university as a teaching fellow in 1952.

Courtesy The Southwest Collection/Special Collections Library, with permission

The difference a year makes: below, the aspiring author at home in November of 1963; at left, the soon-to-be-published novelist in the publicity photo that would appear on Doubleday's 1964 edition of *Walnut Grove.* The latter was taken by Tech Photo in an office at Texas Tech University, where Rushing taught part-time through 1979.

Both photos courtesy James Rushing Jr.

By 1983 Rushing would complete five more novels in the Walnut Grove series, mostly in this writing alcove converted from a guest-room closet. Rushing's son recalls that Rushing "decorated [the alcove] by pasting up all these cut-out reproductions of art works and varnishing them over. . . . I suppose that she wrote everything from *Tamzen* [published in 1972] on in that room, and surely everything except maybe the earliest pages of *Against the Moon* [published in 1968]."

Jane Rushing, circa 1992, on the porch of Harrell Ranch House on the
grounds of the National Ranching Heritage Center, Texas Tech University.
In *Starting from Pryon,* Rushing writes about visiting this house on the
Harrell Ranch, near Camp Springs in Scurry Country, in the early 1970s.
Photograph by James Rushing Jr., with permission.

When asked by Texas Tech University Press for a photo of herself "in her landscape" for the publication of *Starting from Pyron* and the 1992 reissue of *Walnut Grove,* Rushing asked her son James to take a photo at this spot, probably on the grounds of the Lubbock Lake Landmark, which reminded her of Pyron.

➤ Chapter 5 ◆

THE WRITER AND THE
FUNDAMENTALISTS

WITH HER PASSION for opening narrow minds still strong, Rushing soon returned to her manuscript for *The Raincrow*, which she had shelved in 1975 to research and write the history of Texas Tech University with Professor Kline Nall. Again her major thesis examines the hypocrisy of the fundamentalist Protestantism many West Texans practice. The church Rushing describes in *The Raincrow* is often wrongly identified by non-West Texans as the Roman Catholic Church in bibliographic comment and references to the novel. Such a theory is disproved by Rushing in her succinct description of the Church of Christ and its practices in *Starting from Pyron*. Traditionally, Methodists, Baptists, and the Church of Christ have been the chief church builders in West Texas. Roman Catholic churches serve small enclaves, usually of German immigrants on the Rolling Plains, but the Church of Christ dominates.

Although Rushing admits she is not a regular churchgoer, Pat Bennett observes that "[l]ike another serious woman novelist, Shelby Hearon, Rushing uses religion as a major theme in the tapestry of her fiction" (P. Bennett). The driving theme in her last works of fiction reflects Rushing's impatience with unbending adherence to a theology that judges its members on appearance and ignores real social problems in the community. She draws a parallel between the contemporary Church of Christ beliefs and those of the seventeenth-century Puritan church, also called the Church of Christ. The early

church "exhorted Christians to 'love the world with weaned affec-
tions.'" Rushing explains further in *Starting from Pyron* that seventeenth-century theology dictated that

> It is man's duty to pursue with diligence the business of
> this world, to build up an estate for his family, to con-
> tribute to the material needs of his community. Yet bal-
> anced against all this is the abiding concern with the next
> world and the glory of God. As the Boston preacher John
> Cotton wrote, "Such a mystery as none can read but they
> who know it." (III).

Before Rushing explores John Cotton's colonial times, she finished
The Raincrow. Although occurring in modern day Walnut Grove, religious fundamentalism in *The Raincrow* reflects many of the beliefs of
early New England clerics.

The Raincrow (1977)

In Rushing's fifth novel, the narrator Gail Messenger Stoneman
returns to the community that was once Walnut Grove, only to collide
with the church-inspired mores she thought she had escaped when
she left home. In this novel, events take place in the 1970s, a century
after Mary Dove and Red Jones's tragic story, but attitudes in the
community have not changed perceptibly. Gail is a middle-aged,
divorced English professor who returns to her mother's farm to sort
out her problems and to rest during her summer away from the class-
room. Although she does not realize it, she also seeks answers to questions about her family that have troubled her since she fled Walnut
Grove abruptly after high school graduation.

Contributing to the immediacy of this narrative is Gail Stoneman's
first-person, present-tense revelation of her day-to-day activities during her summer visit with her mother. When her memory of personal
history provides the flashbacks necessary for an understanding of her

early departure from Walnut Grove, the author switches to past tense, a technique that involves the reader at once. In an interview, Rushing says she wrote two hundred pages of *The Raincrow* from the omniscient point of view before she perceived she was "not on the right track." She shifted then to the first-person viewpoint with third-person flashbacks, which she says allowed her "to have the main action of the story take place in a short span of time" (Elder 124).

What the narrator hopes to accomplish when she comes home to Walnut Grove is a reconciliation with her mother, Laura Messenger, and a visit with her only son Paul, who is now enthusiastically involved in farming his Grandmother Messenger's farm. Paul has also fallen in love with his second cousin, Cyndi Messenger, daughter of Gail's cousin Stanfield. Gail thinks the visit will heal the carefully unacknowledged and decades-old rift between her and her mother and will bring some peace of mind. She hopes, too, to change Paul's intent to become a farmer. Instead, she suffers from a compulsion to relive her early days in Walnut Grove.

Gail's memories are painful, particularly those concerning her relationship with her mother and their unexplained isolation in the community as she grew up. Her attempt to avoid retracing early unhappy experiences with her cousin Stanfield fails. Only one memory lightens Gail's morose rehash of her life. She is warmed when she thinks of her Grandmother Messenger's comforting presence as she grew up. Mama, as the grandmother was known, cooked superb fried chicken dinners, kept the house, and took care of Gail when she was sick, while Gail's widowed mother went to the fields every day to farm the land Mama had given her. Gail always thought of her grandmother as being one "aspect of mothering," while her mother's role was that of a companion when she took time off from work.

On her first early morning, a bird call stirs a memory that will become a prevalent symbol in the novel and inspires its title. Gail hears a "single hoarse cry . . . repeated several times at intervals." She sorts out her memories, trying to attach a name to the bird's call. She

thinks first of a hound on a hunt: "A strange and mythical hound, lost
like Thoreau's long ago." Then she decides it must be a raincrow, a bird
she has never seen. As a child, she had only heard its call a few times
(13). Nostalgic, she remembers that as an adolescent, when she first
heard the raincrow's cry, she pondered, "What is it really saying?" She
adds, "I remember I tried to write a poem about it and finally gave up,
believing that only if I could interpret the bird's cry would I ever succeed. I wonder if I believe so still" (14). Searching for the elusive bird,
Gail stays on its trail all summer as avidly as Thoreau in his hunt for "a
hound, a bay horse, and a turtle dove." In the end, it is the reader who
understands the symbolic function of this bird, subject of folk superstitions and believed to be harbinger of rainfall. The mysterious raincrow becomes a metaphor for Gail's quest for truth in her memories
of her early life.

Yet another motif apparent in Gail's responses to her native region
captures the bleakness of intellectual life in the now-deserted Walnut
Grove. When her Uncle Hugh, who has almost been a fixture around
the house for many years, visits for the first time after her arrival, they
reminisce about how the community looked in Gail's youth. Gail
recalls the story of the naming of Walnut Grove. She has heard that an
old woman from Tennessee insisted that walnut trees be planted
around the first schoolhouse. Then Gail remembers the rest of the
story—of how the last walnut tree was cut down so a sidewalk could
be built in front of the schoolhouse. Remembering her sometimes
painful adolescence, she thinks, "At that time in my life that act
appeared to me as a symbol of Walnut Grove values." Hugh says he
remembers that when the railroad came through, several citizens
wanted to change the name, but those against change prevailed. The
naysayers argued, significantly and with unconscious irony, that "Walnut Grove was just the name of a place and wasn't supposed to mean
anything" (24). Now, the schoolhouse, the depot, the gin, and the store
have burned or been torn down. Only memories of the farming
Carliles, the storekeeper Baileys, and the presence of the railroad vouch

for the settlement's long-ago existence; but Walnut Grove still serves as the name for the surrounding community. Uncle Hugh remembers hearing that John Carlile, who left Walnut Grove the day it became the name of the town site, is writing a history of the region (65).

Gail will learn by the time she returns home to California that community values during her absence have altered very little. Nevertheless, she finds, too, that time heals old grievances, even in this community where appearances still influence how its citizens treat each other. Soon after her arrival, she accompanies her mother, her son, and her Uncle Hugh when they drive to Stanfield Messenger's modern home in the middle of vast cotton fields for dinner. Stanfield, Hugh's son, occasionally escorted Gail to a movie during their high school days when he needed companionship. The painful memories associated with her relationship with her cousin, now a prosperous farmer, begin to surface that evening and disrupt her peace of mind.

Earlier, in her walk across the farm pasture, Gail considers how they seldom had visitors, as she grew up under the care of her widowed mother and her comfortable Grandmother Messenger. As she grew older, her mother had answered her concern about that with the curt explanation, "It's just our way" (31). She remembers how the community drove away her favorite grade-school teacher, Mr. Thornhill, who told his class about dinosaurs and in the process mentioned the word *evolution*. Brother Jeffcoat, the minister of the church, proclaimed that Thornhill's teaching "is the devil's work at Walnut Grove, and has got to be stopped and stopped fast" (44). Thornhill must go—and he did, almost immediately. At home that day, Gail announces she is glad she did not go to that church, although she knew her mother once was a member. Why they spent Sundays at home has been a mystery, but her mother declares "[i]t was just a question of what they call interpretation that made me stop going to worship. I'm as good a Christian as I ever was, and I aim for you to be. Now I don't want to hear another word about that Mr. Thornhill" (45). Her mother's words do not fully explain why this independent woman, who has raised

Gail and farmed alone with help only from her mother-in-law, has such respect for the church she never attends. The mystery is to be partly solved painfully on the night of Gail's graduation from high school. When she learns what she believes is the truth, Gail also thinks she understands why her childhood has been essentially an isolated life. She has not learned, however, the real reason for her mother's tragic isolation during her childhood.

After high school commencement, where she made the valedictory speech, Gail goes with Stanfield to a dance in a nearby German community. Roughneck boys made bold by alcohol taunt Stanfield with gossip he has never heard. He drags Gail away from the dance, parks, and reveals what he thinks is the truth about his father Hugh's relationship with Gail's mother. They have had an adulterous affair. It all adds up, he tells Gail. His father spends much time with Laura Messenger. She has been thrown out of the church. It is surely more than friendship.

Prelude to Stanfield's disclosure of what he thinks is true about Gail's mother is his abortive attempt to rape Gail. The worst part of that evening, however, is Stanfield's harsh question, "What's the matter with you? Can't you do it like your mother does it?" (163). His explanation of the question dispels Gail's own naiveté. She refuses to listen to her mother's defense of her friendship with Hugh. She leaves soon after for college, never to return home except for brief visits and never, until now, willing to listen to her mother's truthful story of why church members have turned their back to her.

During this visit, Gail at last is able to listen to her mother's version of her personal past history. Laura Messenger has not attended church services since she was formally "issued an ultimatum" by the church many years before, when the church elders declared her guilty of having an affair with her dead husband's brother, Hugh. Accused by Hugh's jealous wife, Estelle, Laura had been given six weeks' grace in which to repent of her sin and correct her behavior. It is true, she tells Gail, that she and Hugh had fallen in love; but theirs was a circumspect, platonic relationship. Laura would not own up to adultery she had not committed. Church members then began to ignore Gail's mother—to "turn their back" on her, as they called it. At the end of her grace period, Laura was "read out" of church membership by the elders.

While Gail copes with the immediate problems of Paul's romance with Stanfield's daughter, Brother Files, the present minister of the church, conspiring with Stanfield and his wife, Tommye Jo, seeks to maneuver Laura's return to the fold. Laura at last capitulates. Gail accompanies her to the service where Laura stands before the congregation while the minister announces that "Sister Laura Messenger confessed that she has sinned against God and Christ's Church and will earnestly try to correct her fault" (269). What Gail does not understand is why her feisty, independent mother does not speak up for herself. Her mother later explains quietly that the Bible says a woman must be silent in church. Gail is indignant, but soon leaves off chastising her mother at her son's insistence. She recognizes how difficult it has been for her mother to stand before church members in the act of confession of a sin she did not commit. Her mother is now back in the good graces of church members. As her mother says, "Nothing else matters."

In this novel, as in the other Walnut Grove novels, the enlightened outsider perceives the anachronistic attitudes of this latter-day frontier community, unwilling to examine the hypocrisy inherent in its values. Representative of the narrow, superficial lives based on appearance that Gail believes her materialistic cousins prefer is their ranch-style brick house, red pickup, yellow Continental, and pink Volkswagen Beetle conspicuously parked in the driveway rather than in the three-car garage. On the day Gail and her family join Stanfield's family for dinner, the pristine lawn surrounding their home in the middle of a vast cotton field impresses Gail. She wonders who takes care of the lawn. Paul tells her to feel it. "My God, it's astroturf," Gail says under her breath (57). The artificial lawn clearly symbolizes to Gail what she as a

snobbish academic believes is the artificiality of her cousins' lives, who she believes value highly the appearance of affluence.

Finally, tempered by the wisdom accumulated through experience, Gail recognizes the good-hearted hospitality of Stanfield and his artificially blond wife, Tommye Jo, as a peace offering. Hugh's vindictive wife Estelle has been dead for years, Stanfield considers his life successful, and the church needs Laura back on its roll. As the community has lost citizens, church membership has also shrunk, and church leaders need her presence every Sunday at Herley, where they now worship. Even the pastor, son of the minister who had turned Gail's mother out of the church so many years ago, says he believes the members' animosity has disappeared. By the time she is ready to return home, Gail accepts her son's love of farming and ambition to make agriculture his life's work. She also is reconciled to the reality of Paul's determination to marry Cyndi. Most significant, however, is that she has learned that what her mother longs for most is not acceptance by the church. Laura has needed the forgiveness of her daughter. In an emotional exchange, Gail vanquishes forever her old grudges against her mother, understanding at last her mother's strength and courage. Gail leaves Walnut Grove with new insight into her own life. She also now understands how heroic her mother's life has been.

Before she leaves for California, Gail once again considers the significance of the raincrow's call during this summer of discovery. When she finds the mysterious bird is only a cuckoo, she is disillusioned. She wanted to attach mythical meaning to the hidden bird. She admits to Paul, "There it was pretending to send me secret messages, and all the time it was really that silly cuckoo, sputtering in the honeysuckle vine" (277). Paul comments, "I sort of thought you felt that way about the raincrow, . . . but after all, how do you know which one is the real bird?" (277). Gail's self-involved questioning leads to few answers, but when she begins to understand that her plaintive personal concerns resemble the silly cuckoo's sputtering in the honeysuckle vine, she at least will go home with some measure of self-understanding.

Early in her visit home, Gail awakens to bird song and "cool honeysuckle air" coming through her open window. She thinks of her own tightly closed house surrounded by a wall with a locked door unopened to her neighbor's garden. In her last conversation with her son, who will remain with his grandmother and farm the land he loves, Gail tells him that when she returns home, she will open that garden gate and invite her neighbors over. Her plan to open the gate seems to imply symbolically that Gail has opened her mind and emotions to others and is finally aware of what havoc her tightly reined emotions have caused her mother and her son.

In an acid-tinged commentary on the state of fiction writing in Texas in 1978, Naomi Lindstrom, a Spanish teacher at the University of Texas, says *The Raincrow* is "a difficult novel for an academically-trained critic to comment upon." She adds, "[I]ndeed, he may feel like an intruder on an alien preserve" ("The Novel in Texas" 82). Obviously steeped in the then new and heady theories of postmodernism, Lindstrom bases her opinions on her reading of the Argentine writer Jorge Luis Borges, who had recently visited the University of Texas campus. In Lindstrom's biographical sketch, she admits "her special interest is literature that, through structural and thematic means, seeks to confront the reader with the irrational, the disordered, and the incoherent." Praising two writers of whom little has been heard since her article was published, Lindstrom takes to task not only Rushing's novel, but also Shelby Hearon's *A Prince of a Fellow* and Elmer Kelton's *The Good Old Boys* for their blatant regionalism and "absence of novelistic innovation." The critic, inadvertently it would seem, points out the strength of Rushing's novel when she says, "The author has evidently taken the greatest pains to furnish an accurate mock-up of local landscape, customs, speech, and manners. However, the real focus is not on this painstakingly worked-out backdrop, but on the human drama that takes place against it." She adds, "*The Raincrow* is not written for people who have a special interest in the novel as such but for those who care about characters and care about them rather as though they were human beings" (82). Clearly for Lindstrom, *The Raincrow* was much too rational, orderly, and coherent to convey great truths; her assessment is a scholarly attack on regionalism, a fashionable stance among members of the academy as far back as the 1920s.

Reviewer Hazel Richardson gets closer to the significance of Rushing's novel in her informed appraisal. For Richardson the novelist's aim with its strong sense of place is to discover the truth. Richardson judges that the novel is "not a story of suspense or dramatic confrontations. It is a story of understanding in human relationships, especially family relationships." She praises the author for "her ability to make the West Texas scene speak for all the world and its inhabitants for all people." That ability has proved to be one of Rushing's strengths as a writer. Richardson concludes by proclaiming Rushing a major Southwestern writer. In his 1982 interview of the author for the *Dallas Morning News*, Patrick Bennett identifies yet another strength of this writer when he says *The Raincrow* is an "iceberg novel" and "the most subtle and psychologically complex" work the author has written ("Jane Rushing," February 14, 1982).

Daryl Jones's afterword to *Starting from Pyron* points out that this novel brings the Walnut Grove works "full circle" in Rushing's fictional examination of the regional history she knows so well. Jones says, "Considered as a whole, Jane Gilmore Rushing's West Texas novels create a fictive world that owes its very substance to the rich store of source materials and experiences recollected in *Starting from Pyron*" (151). Published as a *Redbook* novel in the July 1977 issue of the magazine, *The Raincrow* was also named an alternate selection by the Book-of-the-Month Club.

The Raincrow, set in contemporary times, logically concludes Rushing's fictional examination of her native region; but in the 1980s, she would publish yet another novel and a novella in which she earnestly examines the consequences in West Texas communities of hidden wrongdoing and community censorship of appearance, often while they ignore the truth. By the late 1970s, however, Rushing was ready to create the historical novel she had thought about writing for some time.

Covenant of Grace (1982)

Early in 1982, after interviewing Rushing at her home, Patrick Bennett's feature story, "Jane Rushing: Mixing Religion, Writing," came out in the *Dallas Morning News*. The occasion for their conversation was Doubleday's imminent release of Rushing's sixth novel, *Covenant of Grace*. Bennett reports that the novelist pointed out "right off that she doesn't think of her new puritan New England novel as a radical departure from her West Texas books." Rushing proves her point in this, her longest novel. With her knowledge of early colonial life acquired after several years of intensive research, Rushing recaptures the life of Anne Hutchinson, whose charismatic personality and devout belief in salvation through grace led finally to her banishment from the Massachusetts Bay Colony in 1638.

In "Setting in the Historical Novel," Rushing discusses at length the process that led to writing *Covenant of Grace*. Published in *The Writer* in 1984, Rushing's essay considers this novel to be her only historical fiction. She labels her West Texas novels her "period pieces," faithful to time and place but with invented plot and character. For this latest novel, she reconstructs the lives of prominent players in early American history after she spent much time investigating the colonial period. Reading the work of the early colonial poet Anne Bradstreet inspired Rushing to begin research into the life and times of colonial society. She soon knew she wanted to narrate Anne Hutchinson's story after reading journals and diaries created for the researcher a "fuller sense of time and place." For Rushing, the valuable journal of John Winthrop, published as the *History of New England*,

gave her further insight into the Puritan's belief that everyday happenings are often signs from God. In her discussion of the origins of
this novel, Rushing also provides her most cogent denial that she
meant to portray Anne Hutchinson as an early advocate of women's
rights. Warning against interpreting the past in "terms of modern
ideas," she admits that when she first began planning to write about
Anne Hutchinson, she thought she might find her an early promoter
of women's rights. But after extensive research into Anne's life, Rushing says she was unable to discover any desire on Anne Hutchinson's
part to change women's roles in colonial society. Rushing believes as a
"brave, intelligent woman, she may serve as an inspiration to all
women who fight for a cause, but to present her as a seventeenth-century feminist would be an anachronism" (14–15).

When the reader meets Anne Hutchinson in *Covenant of Grace*, she
is shepherding her large family off the ship *Arbella*, which has just
arrived in the Boston Harbor in September 1634. She has persuaded
her businessman husband William that following her beloved preacher
and mentor, John Cotton, to the four-year-old colony would be a
good move for the whole family. Already aware of the harshness of a
religion emphasizing the penalties of sin over the grace of God,
Anne's sometimes outspoken support of salvation by grace on the
journey over has irritated Reverend Zachariah Symmes, who has
delivered sermons on board. Almost before her household is settled,
she is called before Symmes. John Cotton and Pastor John Wilson
gathered at Cotton's house, where Anne is asked to answer sharp
questions about her beliefs. She is straightforward in explaining her
opinion that persons are saved only through grace and acceptance of
an indwelling Christ as the Holy Spirit. Her inquisitors insist she
explain how she feels about the role of works in proving one's assur-
ance of salvation. She explains that works are important but not the
main standard by which to judge a Christian. When she puts Cotton
on the defensive by referring to his previous teachings, which she
believes validate her beliefs, the respected theologian admits he has

shared her attitude toward the covenant of grace; but he obviously is uneasy in the presence of this articulate woman. Anne's belief is that

> It was an easy, simple doctrine Cotton taught. . . . Not by
> good works does a man reach salvation, nor by any
> thought he can take, but by union with Christ which
> comes only through the grace of God. The assurance
> constantly sought by every Christian could be found
> through his awareness of this union, the sense of the Holy
> Ghost within. (22)

His fellow clerics think of the covenant of grace as counter to their emphasis on works as the way to salvation, so Cotton, who needs their good will to succeed in his work in the colony, must balance his high regard for Anne with his desire for influence among colonial leaders, all preachers. After private consultation, the ministers tell Anne they will recommend that the ruling elders accept her profession of faith so that she can become a member of the church. "If I ask for it," she thinks as she leaves (45).

Anne soon discovers her every move is monitored by John Winthrop, as self-appointed keeper of the morals of the colony and Massachusetts Bay Colony's former governor. She creates uneasiness among the elders right away when she is asked by women acquaintances to begin teaching sessions in her home, where she explains in her clear voice the words of Sunday morning preachers and Sunday afternoon teachers, whose ideas are often obscure to their congregation. She sits regally in her home's main room in her great wainscot chair with its high carved back, the one piece of furniture that had belonged to her revered and scholarly father, where she speaks at length after much meditation to growing crowds of women, who find her religious theories understandable and attractive. Within a few months, both men and women are gathering weekly in the Hutchinson home. Soon, Anne Hutchinson, charismatic and persuasive, finds herself the unaware instigator of the Antinomian Controversy, which threatened the Puritan preachers' autonomy.

Historically a crisis in the Massachusetts Bay community in the 1640s, the controversy focused on Anne Hutchinson's teachings, which held that acceptance of Christ's grace would lead to right action, not according to one's own will, but through the presence of the Holy Ghost within those who believed. The implication in what she taught led her followers to place little emphasis on moral responsibility, because they believed the Holy Ghost within dictated their actions. Hutchinson's beliefs obviously were more emotional than logical. Her adversaries believed justification of the saved led to a believer's demonstrating his faith through right living and good works. Hutchinson's teachings soon led to condemnation by the ruling theocracy and their declaration that her beliefs deserved the charge of heresy.

Meanwhile, although she has said works do not open the gates of Heaven, Anne Hutchinson becomes known as a competent midwife and nurse to the ill. Frequently called upon, Anne's companion on these missions is the little hunchback Goody Jane Hawkins, who has established a reputation as dispenser of exotic herbs meant to heal. In her description of the personalities and activities of women who live on the margin of society, as Goody Hawkins does, Rushing humanizes the life of this long-ago, and often mythologized, society. One of the most poignant stories is that of Jacob Hickson, a bond servant released by a poverty-stricken bondsman, and Elizabeth Joan, who has run away from an abusive stepfather. When Anne is called out the first time to assist Goody Hawkins, it is to deliver Elizabeth Joan's baby. Anne remembers seeing this young couple standing on the town scaffold on lecture day with the letter *F* pinned to their backs. She knows that identifies them as fornicators, caught in the act of lovemaking without benefit of marriage. Later, they marry. Now Elizabeth Joan's life is in danger. Anne and Jane deliver the dead baby and provide care and food until the young girl recovers. Then despite Jacob's dislike of the two women, Elizabeth Joan is invited to work for Anne, helping with her many children.

When Jacob launches his boat into a still-icy sea, John Winthrop, ever alert to all the actions of what he considers to be his flock, tries to stop his sailing out into sure disaster. Jacob, who knows he and Elizabeth Joan are sure to starve if he does not fish, shocks the busybody John Winthrop with his retort: "How is it that every god-damn-me in Boston knows what every honest man is doing every minute of the day? . . . Have you wrote down every time we piss and every time we shit?" (68). After Winthrop vows to take care of this blasphemer if God does not, the narrator continues with this commentary: "Jacob might have been more nearly right than he suspected when he taunted this man. Sooner or later, John Winthrop knew everything that happened in Boston. And when it was evil, either God or Winthrop meted out the proper punishment" (69).

With her understanding of human conduct and desire, Rushing creates characters in this narrative who both profit from Anne Hutchinson's controversial teachings and twist her theology to support their selfish aims. For the simple Goody Hawkins, it is a struggle to make sense of her beloved Anne's teachings. When Anne asks Jane if she understands what she is saying, Jane always answers that she does; but in truth, she struggles with what are for her troublesome concepts. Jane's dilemma begins with her simple interpretation of Ann's words:

> Anyone at all—anyone in the world, . . . can hope to go
> to heaven. You don't have to do anything, Christ just
> comes to you, out of His great love, and joins Himself to
> you. . . . Jane had the greatest difficulty imagining any
> portion of Christ anywhere inside her own bony chest—
> but where else could he be? She never asked Anne
> Hutchinson about that, never asked anything much; she
> had the feeling of delicacy about Anne's beliefs, as if too

much probing would expose something hard and rocky
that a person like Jane would have to stumble over, or a
pit for her to fall into. . . . [When Anne asks Jane if her
teachings are clear], at the time, it always did seem so, as if
nothing in the world would ever be easier and clearer
than the love of God. It was only afterward, walking some
lonely path by the seashore, that she would see there must
be something else she didn't understand—some trick
to it. (82)

Jane, uneducated and naive, reflects in her confusion on what
Rushing obviously perceives as the negatives associated with Anne
Hutchinson's teachings. The clever Captain John Underhill, the lecher-
ous, egotistical commander of the colony's militia, prefers a simplistic
interpretation of Anne's words. Although married, he sees that Elizabeth Joan, now widowed, is a likely conquest. She is lonely and obviously approachable. She agrees to meet him in the isolated hovel she
and Jacob occupied before his death. To rationalize his adultery, the
married Underhill finds comfort in Anne's teachings. He knows the
sin of adultery is punishable by death, but he knows of no one who has
yet died for that sin in the colony. From questioning his wife Helena
after she has attended one of Anne's meetings, he has come to the conclusion that "the God who made us would understand our weaknesses,
and that when He sent Christ to save us, He would save us, weaknesses
and all" (107). With the subtle wit that is a Rushing trademark, the narrator describes the pompous Underhill as having established his own
rules for such conduct: he would never touch a virgin, never get
involved with a prostitute, and never get involved with a woman with
no husband to father any child she might conceive.

He breaks his third rule with Elizabeth Joan, and she almost loses
her life after Goody Hawkins performs a primitive abortion. Anne is
called to help save the young woman's life, where she also assures Elizabeth Joan she is still God's child. In a scene reminiscent of Edna's

determined march into the Gulf in Kate Chopin's turn-of-the-century novel, *The Awakening* (1899), the distraught Elizabeth Joan eventually walks out into the sea to her death, believing Christ is calling her. The reader is made to experience her agony as she almost mindlessly wades into the surf.

The next day, John Wilson declares in his Sunday sermon that "he was thankful the lewd girl had been struck down in the midst of her sinful life and so sent straight to hell." Anne Hutchinson walks out. At the gathering in her home next day, she defends this girl whom she has loved "with a fierceness none had ever seen in her before" (165). What Rushing accomplishes in her moving narration of human tragedy resulting from the harsh demands of orthodoxy is the creation of characters with dimension and substance. Textbook history intent on recording dates and events becomes in Rushing's novel a vivid chronicling of the everyday lives of unique individuals, weak and strong, who became entangled in the Antinomian Controversy.

Inevitably, interested men begin to join the women who gather regularly to hear Anne's teachings. Among them is a young and handsome new arrival from England who becomes enchanted with Anne as both a woman and teacher. Only twenty-two, Henry Vane, son of the comptroller of King Charles's household and a dissenter, is welcomed in the colony, particularly by its leaders. His connections in England may prove valuable to the renewal of the colony's charter. Soon, he is living at John Cotton's house and spending his spare hours talking to Anne. Anne has found an ally with passion. Her husband William is an up-and-coming merchant of fine fabrics; and although he loves Anne intensely, he sees an advantage in not irritating John Winthrop, John Cotton, Thomas Dudley, or John Wilson by questioning their beliefs and leadership. He quietly supports and encourages Anne, but he remains low-key in the matter of discussing religious tenets. He is, however, finally confronted by John Winthrop, who threatens when he says, "Sir, if you do not begin to control your wife, you may have the dissolution of the colony to answer for." William sees this as a warning, but he knows he does not ever intend to attempt control of Anne's religious life. However, Anne's gentle husband wonders "if she had ever questioned whether God meant her to use up her whole strength and call down upon herself the wrath of the ministers and magistrates. For was this God's only truth, this truth she preached?" (211).

Soon, Anne spends more time in planning strategy to combat her now acknowledged enemies than in meditation. She has become uncharacteristically angry and vengeful in her thoughts and even her teaching after John Winthrop, who lives across the Boston high street from the Hutchinson home, drives from her doorstep a distraught young woman seeking Anne's help. Later, the young woman, mad from uncertainty over her salvation, throws her baby into a well, in order, she tells her husband, that she can be certain she is damned. She is hanged. That day Anne becomes more politician than teacher. She is determined to defeat the likes of John Winthrop, who rules the colony's everyday life with a heavy hand. Her first overt act of rebellion is to lead her followers from the meetinghouse any time she disagrees with John Wilson's preaching.

Political concerns begin to overshadow religious life in Boston and surrounding villages as well. Indian uprisings lead Henry Vane, now the young and inept governor of the colony, to work for a new treaty with the Pequod and Narragansett tribes. Many see the need for an institute of higher learning yet the leaders know knowledge leads to questioning accepted belief. Citizens become more and more contentious over both religious and political issues. In truth, separating civic concerns from the church's influence is impossible. John Winthrop has visualized "a city on the hill," illuminating the New World with the light of moral uprightness. John Cotton, up to this time ambiguous in stating his religious beliefs, has come to see he can no longer hide behind his famous defense that his belief in both salvation through grace and sanctification by works is only different "a narrow scantling" from Winthrop's and Wilson's. He now, however, "felt like a fish somehow caught in two nets by two fishermen at the same time" (183).

Soon, women in Anne's camp begin to speak up during sermons and question the preacher's opinions. Men eventually join the contentious women. John Winthrop writes in his journal: "Now . . . the faithful ministers of Christ must have dung cast on their faces, and be no better than legal preachers, Baal's priests, Popish factors, scribes, Pharisees, and opposers of Christ himself" (qtd. in *Covenant* 235). Although Cotton pushes for compromise between Winthrop's supporters and Hutchinson's "opinionists," it is soon clear to Anne's friends that he, too, will surrender to political expediency.

Finally, John Winthrop becomes governor again, a position giving him an advantage politically, even though many in Boston no longer support his narrow and harsh views. Nevertheless, he sees to the passage of a law "prohibiting any newcomer from staying more than three weeks in the colony without the approval of two magistrates or one member of the Council for Life" (262). Because Winthrop is a member of the Council for Life, he can turn away any new arrival without any other citizen's approval. He generously, some observe bitterly, allows some of Anne's newly arrived kin to stay four months. The family puzzles over why Winthrop decides they cannot be welcomed as citizens after questioning them. Anne decides their error is in being her relatives. Her husband's cousin Samuel even sees humor in their rejection. He says he did seem to irritate Winthrop when he said the heat in Boston was unlike any he had ever experienced. Rushing may have meant to imply a double meaning in criticizing "the heat in Boston." Certainly, the modern slang usage of "feeling the heat" was precisely what those associated with Anne Hutchinson began to experience. Samuel and his family decide to settle elsewhere in the colonies.

Finally in the fall of 1636, John Winthrop orders Anne Hutchinson before the civil court to explain the opinions he and the preachers in the colonies believe are heretical, and clearly he also perceives her beliefs as threatening to the preachers' autocratic positions in the colony. After long hours of interrogation, Anne is banished from Boston and ordered to leave by March 1637. Until that time, she is imprisoned in the home of a Newtown preacher, where she suffers from loneliness, physical problems, and finally doubt in her own beliefs. Her last ordeal is the trial before the church congregation, where in the end she is excommunicated, a far worse sentence to Anne than being thrown out of the colony. Betrayed by her revered John Cotton, whose teaching back in England had inspired her family's move to the Bay Colony, she comes to see the true motive for John Winthrop's and Thomas Dudley's hatred of her. She suddenly realizes

> None of them was thinking nearly as much about the
> welfare of her soul as about his ambitions for himself, and
> for the colony as he conceived it. Winthrop had a vision
> of a city upon a hill; so doubtless, did they all. And in the
> shining streets of that city, there was no place for Anne
> Hutchinson. (384)

As she looks into the hard eyes of her inquisitors, she admits to herself that she has been on the verge of confessing to beliefs she did not hold in order to remain in this church. She is horrified when she suddenly comprehends that "[f]or the sake of something called a church, and forgetting that her covenant was with God instead of men, she had been about to deny herself and Christ. She thanked God silently; and the records show she never spoke another word till the Boston church was done with her" (384).

Because Anne loves those who come to her for help, much of what the preachers condemn her for is not her beliefs, as they seem to be saying. Her compassion comforts such women as Goody Jane Hawkins, ultimately accused of being a witch, because the child Mary Dyer conceived with the aid of her herbs and medicines arrives in seven months, stillborn and deformed. Winthrop learns of the deformed child, which John Cotton has quietly helped William and Anne Hutchinson bury in order to save Mary from the sure opinion that the child must have been the result of Mary's consorting with a witch. He will later use that knowledge to turn public opinion against Anne. It is Mary Dyer who joins Anne in her long walk out of the meetinghouse after her excommunication.

John Cotton, several years later, informs his congregation of the final tragedy in Anne's life—not in sympathy but as an example of the destiny a heretical woman must suffer. He describes in gory detail Anne's murder and burning by Indians on Long Island Sound, where she had settled with her children after her husband William died in Rhode Island. He furnishes graphic detail of how Anne's family is attacked and massacred. Anne, he says, had died at a place called Hell-Gate on the map. He concludes, "Thus we see God's wondrous ways in putting an end to that most satanic life on earth." Rising from her seat, a woman in the gray cloak and hat that Mary Dyer always wore, walks to the middle of the aisle, turns and faces Cotton. "May the Lord forgive you, John Cotton," she says. "No woman who loved Anne Hutchinson ever will" (389).

In her essay discussing how she prepared to write this novel, Rushing warns future writers of historical fiction that characterization obviously must be true to the time and place in which the novel is set. For this novel, she read widely and consulted the *Oxford English Dictionary* and writings of the time in order to capture the exact language of the 1600s. She studied court transcripts. She also found that most of what had been written about Anne Hutchinson during her lifetime was written by her enemies. Her challenge then was to imagine a charismatic woman leader whose stubborn adherence to her beliefs could cause such an uproar in colonial Boston.

In this novel, Rushing demonstrates great talent for depicting human personality with the characteristics most consider universal as well as those traits and actions peculiar to early American colonists. In the Council's intensive questioning, an inquisition that led to Anne's banishment, Rushing captures the emotions of both the inquisitors and of Anne as she bravely stands her ground against these formidable men. Anne's anguish leads to uncharacteristic weeping when she is sentenced to imprisonment and separation from her children. She "broke at last." After her friend Mary Dyer comforts her when vivid images of her children at home crowd into her imagination, she regains her composure and walks "erect and tall" as she is escorted away by a marshal dressed in black, to months of near total isolation (331).

With *Covenant of Grace*, Rushing established her credentials as a novelist worthy of serious critical attention. Robert Compton, then book editor of the *Dallas Morning News,* sent Jane a clipping of Judith Eubank's lengthy review, which was published as lead essay in the Sunday *News* book pages with the banner headline "Healer or Heretic? The Story of Anne Hutchinson." Appearing on June 6, 1982, the essay praises Rushing's restraint as she takes care "that her imagined people and incidents pay off in a more focused, resonant narrative." Eubank says Rushing's careful prose avoids any technique that would sensationalize Anne Hutchinson's predicament. She notes that the author avoids overuse of invented detail, any attitude of moral outrage, or the presentation of the protagonist "as the spirited yet pitiable victim of male oppression." The result, according to the reviewer, is a tragic story; but "Rushing won't let it dwindle into melodrama."

Rushing wrote Pat Bennett about how pleased she was with Eubank's appraisal (June 15, 1982). She may have particularly approved of the reviewer's judgment that her portrayal of this seventeenth-century woman is not as a victim of male oppression but as an unorthodox citizen whose views threatened unity of the colony. As she would say later in *The Writer,* "I could never see that she (or anyone in the world she knew) was concerned with changing the position of women. Because she is a brave, intelligent woman, she may serve as inspiration to all women who fight for a cause, but to present her as a seventeenth-century feminist would be an anachronism" ("Setting" 15).

Despite Rushing's denial that she intended to write a defense of feminism, Rice University professor Susan Clark argues in the *Texas Observer* (August 6, 1982) that "Rushing's own powerful depiction of Anne as one who did not draw distinctions, as one who educates women (and men alike), and as one who leads her followers in walking out of church where unpure doctrine is propounded . . . marks Anne as a feminist, whether she realizes it or not." She concludes, "Rushing may not be aware of how truly feminist her portrayal of Anne is. *Covenant of Grace* treats an uncommonly strong, intelligent woman whose life, in this well-written biographical novel, comes vividly alive. Rushing's work is a fine addition to an increasing body of works focusing on women's history" (20).

The author never concedes that she has meant to create Anne Hutchinson as a feminist rebel. What she aimed to do, she says two years later, is "build a character who could satisfactorily account for a controversy that all but wrecked a colony and has appealed to every generation down to modern times—almost in the form of myth" ("Setting" 15).

That Rushing returned to her native West Texas for the setting of her next novel is not surprising. Changing settings and time does not necessarily lead to change of theme, however. In his interview with the writer, Pat Bennett reports that "[s]he said right off that she doesn't think of her puritan New England novel as a radical departure from her West Texas books." Rushing adds, "There are many parallels. . . . The climate, for instance, is not the same but in both cases it is harsh and demanding." She continues, "And the people who settled West Texas, the farming people, weren't precisely puritans, but they were fundamentalists in their religious thinking, and their thoughts and morals were a lot like the puritans" ("Jane Rushing" 1982)

Winds of Blame (1983)

With the theme that stitches all of her novels into a social history exhibiting the same patterns of community attitudes, Rushing began writing her seventh and last novel, *Winds of Blame*, soon after the manuscript of *Covenant of Grace* was in press at Doubleday. John Winthrop and his cohorts dealt immediate judgment on those whose lives apparently did not follow their strict code of what appearances should be in their "city on a hill," while they themselves harbored hatred and dealt out cruel punishments to those who did not conform to their rules. Not too different in *Winds of Blame* are the attitudes of the moral arbiters in the Rolling Plains community of Greenfields, when in 1916 a desperate family conspires to rid themselves of a despot father. In their efforts to conceal the truth of their failure to rescue the abused wife and family who find themselves in hopeless circumstances, leaders in the Greenfield church choose instead to judge the "looks of the thing," which leads finally to tragedy none can ignore.

In the prologue to *Winds of Blame*, the narrator identifies herself only as the granddaughter of Joanna Waters Doane, one of two women whose lives and friendship become the focus of the novel's plot. Earlier the narrator has collected community lore for an oral history project assigned by the teacher of her college folklore class. In the words of this young woman who has become intrigued with the stories she has heard, Rushing herself makes clear why fiction such as hers yields an understanding of the development of a major cultural group in the West. In her explanation of why she felt compelled to tell the story of the tragic Doane family, the narrator begins:

> I may as well say at the outset that this is a story of guns
> and trouble. It is not exactly a story of the Old West,
> although in the teen years of the century . . . [T]he part of
> Texas where I live had not outgrown its frontier ways. I

used to think this lingering wildness had something to do
with what happened in the Doane family, but I'm not so
sure now. The Doane story is part of our folklore and
therefore once seemed to me peculiar to the community
of Greenfields; but I have found out it involves a kind of
violence not much limited by time or space. . . . The truth
is a hard thing to know . . . but I am convinced I can
come close to it, for I have heard the events narrated
many times, and during the last years of my grandmother's life I questioned her closely about them. I have
also had access to diaries and letters that speak to me
directly from the past. (3)

The storyteller adds that after moving to Greenfields and hearing
more of her Grandmother's stories, she felt she had "finally seen *Oedipus the King* performed, after reading only the prose summary of it in
some book of myths for children" (4). She decides to tell the story of
this community tragedy with all of its implications as a tribute to the
courage and loyalty of her grandmother and her grandmother's girlhood friend Isabel, sister of Ray Doane, whom Joanna married.

Joanna is the daughter of Martha Waters, who is warmhearted but
abides by long-set rules for conducting her life and supervising that of
her family. Isabel, who is often in the Waters home, "did not see anything paradoxical in the strictness with which Mrs. Waters regulated
the life of her family as compared with her own sense of freedom
when she came into that open, sunlit house" (48–49). Mrs. Waters's
close monitoring of the girls' activities does not affect Isabel's pleasure
when she visits Joanna; she has escaped for a little while her father's
cruel oppression of the Doane family. The explanation for Isabel's
unquestioning acceptance of Mrs. Waters's many rules of proper conduct recalls Rushing's observation that there are distinct parallels in
the rules for living that both Puritans and West Texans followed without examination. The narrator observes that even small exceptions to

rules, such as Mrs. Waters sitting down in the middle of the afternoon to enjoy a piece of cake, surprises her family. Predictability of actions and responses of community adults in some ways provide a secure environment for Greenfields' young. The narrator points out the advantages of knowing the rules:

> [S]uch regularity was simply the basis of society in
> Greenfields, as in every community and rural town across
> a wide expanse of western plain and prairie. It underlay
> every category of their lives, and no one questioned the
> rules. There might from time to time be found someone
> to darkly circumvent them; but no one questioned them.
> They concerned order in families, the ethics of horse-
> breaking, the opening and closing of wire gates (leave the
> gate the way you found it), the music permitted at parties
> (group singing—no fiddles)—a hundred matters big and
> small, but nothing more serious and fundamental (noth-
> ing more surely common to every place) than the rules of
> sex, mainly as it pertained to the behavior of courting
> couples, but also (rare in the sense that it was mostly con-
> cealed) the straying of a married man or woman. (49)

As Rushing's readers have learned, like the nearby settlement of Walnut Grove, Greenfields is a community where appearance takes precedence over truth. Martha Waters, Joanna's mother, is a paragon of housewifely virtue. She often warns her daughter she must be care-ful of her behavior with Ray Doane, lest the community's keepers of moral uprightness draw the wrong conclusions about their rela-tionship.

Joanna's friend Isabel is the oldest daughter of Harvey Doane, a tyrant. It is an unacknowledged truth that Harvey Doane has crippled his wife and physically abuses his children. Isabel is to learn, too, that he has also sexually used her twelve-year-old sister Sophie. The story begins with Harvey following Isabel as she joins Joanna to walk to the wedding of her teacher, Miss Lona Miller. He orders her home with the lame excuse that she should be caring for her mother. Jerking the sash she wears pinned with a red rose from her waist, he says, "I don't recollect giving anybody permission to deck theirself out like a dance-hall girl and go traipsing down the road picking flowers" (11).

The soon-to-be-married Miss Lona's characterization is based on memories of an early teacher at Pyron. Rushing describes Miss Lona Miller (her real name) in *Starting from Pyron* as perhaps "the prettiest teacher Pyron ever had." Her Grandmother Adams remembered her as a community favorite (61). She is depicted in the novel as wise and observant. When she learns why her favorite student Isabel is not at the wedding, Miss Lona admonishes Joanna in the privacy of her bedroom, "You must get Isabel away from there. . . . She must not be trapped in that house, with that evil man" (20). Miss Lona has encouraged both girls to follow her to East Texas, where they can enroll in the college where her husband-to-be is a professor and study for certification as schoolteachers. She confuses Joanna, however, with her harsh judgment of Harvey Doane, whose actions as head of the family have not been questioned by the community. Joanna is shocked at the intensity of Miss Lona's command. When the teacher sees her confusion, she reassures Joanna by saying she had gone too far, but she nevertheless meant what she has said.

Miss Lona sees the truth behind appearance, but she is leaving Greenfields. Those left behind would not agree for several more months with this young teacher's judgment of Harvey Doane as an evil menace. There is no public censorship of Harvey Doane because he keeps up appearances, as the biblically ordained head of the household, by regularly attending church. Doane's cruelty to his family may stir up murmured criticism but never interference in his family affairs. It is after all the "looks-of-the-thing" that counts.

Doane's cruel acts escalate. He drives his sons as though they are slaves. Isabel realizes her mother Lizzie is becoming more passive, fear-

ful, and withdrawn. Finally Harvey makes a fatal mistake. He brings
the prostitute, Alma Greeping, home and installs her in a dugout near
the house. Ray calls a family conference when Harvey and Alma are
away. That day they decide killing Harvey Doane is the only solution
to their terrible dilemma. They are desperately afraid of this irrational,
cruel man, and they know the community will not intercede. Only
Isabel objects to this violent solution, which she foresees will bring
only more trouble to the doomed family. The second of two
epigraphs prefacing the novel, which repeats the words of Pope John
Paul II, becomes relevant here: "The truth is not always the same as
majority opinion." What Isabel intuitively understands is that, in this
case, majority opinion ignores the consequences of committing patri-
cide. For her, murder, even of a cruel father, is morally wrong, no matter what the circumstances; and she foresees rightly that such an act
will lead to an even more tragic aftermath. She enjoys the Waters's
pleasant home life and wonders often why her home is such an
unhappy place. She thinks perhaps the fundamental principle contributing to a happy family life is "a sense of proportion and order,
under some sort of law based on reason and love" (60).

All of Harvey Doane's children have reasons to despise him, particularly Ray, who as the oldest son, feels the heaviest responsibility
for his neglected mother, Lizzie, who has been crippled for several
years after Harvey whipped up the horses as she was getting into the
buggy. Adolescent Burnie is crippled as well because Harvey Doane
drove away a doctor who might have delivered the child sooner and
prevented permanent physical injury to the boy. After all of the family
except Isabel agrees to Harvey's murder, she recalls for her older
brother that the commandment says "Thou shalt not kill." She
secretly thinks, too, that her father has not always been the cruel man
he has become, when she remembers that during her early years her
father talked and laughed with the family around the table. For Isabel
his tyranny over the family became more evident after his horse farm
failed and he lost part of his land. He had always denigrated the "dirt

farmer" and had dreamed of establishing a horse ranch here in the West like his grandfather's back in East Texas. This oldest daughter admits "he had become what he had always been, but there was a time when his wife and children did not live with a sense of impending reasonless violence" (22). She urges restraint, reminding the family that if the law cannot solve their problem, God surely will.

Ray points out she is only one among seven. The majority rules. Isabel, still hopeful her brother will examine the consequences of murder, says she has heard that one person can hang a jury. Ray says this is not a jury. Isabel warns one more time: "Let me just say one more thing, Ray, . . . I'm afraid you're headed for bad trouble. And yet— I can't tell what will happen—I guess you might go free. But even if you do, you'll be known for the rest of your life, and you'll know yourself, as the man that killed his father" (127). Ray's only answer is "So be it."

A few mornings later, Harvey is found dead where he was crossing a fence carrying a gun. Without audible agreement, the neighbors choose at once to believe Doane's murder is accidental. Most admit privately they think Ray Doane shot his father. Much to their relief, the justice of peace declares that Harvey has accidentally shot himself, even though Ray confesses he is responsible. For the community this act and the lawman's conclusion solve the problem of the Doane family. When Justice of Peace Goolsby rules on the death, he declares:

> I've just got to use the evidence of my own eyes . . . and
> my ruling is this case is accidintal [*sic*] death. It's plumb
> clear what happened. He was crawling over the fence
> with a loaded gun in his hand. I am sure he knew better,
> but the wisest of us can be careless sometimes. . . . It was a
> sad accidint, [*sic*]. . . And that's my ruling: that no blame be
> attached to anyone alive. (133)

With this verdict, it is plain that Justice Goolsby's intent is to absolve the community as well as the family of guilt. Here the relevancy to both the theme and title of a second epigraph quoted from *Hamlet* becomes clear: "And for his death, no wind of blame shall breathe, / But even his mother shall uncharge the practice, / And call it accident" (IV, vii)

Isabel records her secret opinions of life around her in her journal. With her writer's need to analyze her family's tragedy, she knows this will not be the end of the matter. Nevertheless, as Sam Flowers told young John Carlile in *Walnut Grove*, "They think as long as they don't say it, it's not true" (215). Greenfields people judge right living by those same terms. They stick to their story when outsiders begin to ask questions; but tragedy inherent in even the "good lie," as one astute young citizen calls falsehood told to save feelings, soon touches the lives of many. A community crisis erupts.

Jack Waters, Joanna's older, free-thinking brother, opens her mind to the possibility that her fiancé has killed his father. He points out first that up until recently, Harvey Doane was "a man of the community," the head of his family, and that all of the men in the community actually liked him until he showed up at church with Alma. Jack adds that for those reasons, "[W]hat he did at home was not really anybody's business." Joanna comprehends now that Jack is trying to tell her calling the murder an accident will only cause problems for Ray. Jack assures his sister he does not want to bring trouble on Ray, but he wonders if "everything might be better in the long run if folks didn't always try to cover up the truth." Almost in tears, Joanna gains her brother's sympathy; and he tries to comfort her, "You're all right, Jo, . . . [a]nd who am I to say the looks of the thing is not the same as the truth?" (141)

Joanna's mother, aware she will not be able to keep Joanna and Ray from seeing each other, exacts a promise, however, that they will wait until Ray's life is more settled before they marry. Further complications occur when young Archie Hastings, a reporter for the county paper, the *Western Messenger,* begins to look into Harvey's death. Shortly, he and Isabel recognize that they are very much attracted to each other. Greenfields citizens know Archie is on a quest for the truth. Gossiping tongues begin to speculate and disapproval becomes visible when Isabel and Archie are seen driving around the country-side. It is Jack Waters again who this time warns Isabel that commu-nity opinion is beginning to censure her actions. He says the commu-nity gossips know her relationship with the reporter is innocent. He adds, "But they've got their damn looks-of-the-thing so mixed up with the truth that they think it's worse for you to get out of sight somewhere with him than it was for Ray to kill his daddy" (250).

Isabel, sensing that this astute, young journalist is close to exposing the town lie and learning the truth of her father's death, asks him not to return. Her crippled brother Burnie has become hostile to Archie as well. The community is relieved at first. They have secretly feared he would expose their mutual dissembling, which they cannot admit means they are protecting a murderer. Although Isabel has found talk-ing to Archie about books and ideas has given her a glimpse of what it might mean to accept Miss Lona's offer to help her go to college, she knows his journalist's need to discover the whole story will finally result in his discovery that her brother is a murderer. She is warned by his curiosity on the day she shows him around their farm, and they climb into the barn loft. Archie has questions about an empty rifle shell he finds there.

Despite her promise to her brothers and her estrangement from Joanna because of their fears, Isabel writes Archie, telling him she needs to see him. As he has done once before, Joanna's father, who is postmaster as well as store owner, intercepts her letters, breaking the law without guilt to protect the community's reputation. Jack Waters reveals to Isabel that his father has been holding letters Archie has written her. The terrible realization comes to Isabel that these people she has known all of her life aim to cover up her brother's act by shift-

ing their critical focus to her relationship with Archie. She comes to
the devastating conclusion that in this community "nothing had
changed. Life would still be lived by Greenfields truth." With courage
fueled by her desperation, she decides to face the community in
church on Sunday.

When the sanctimonious Sunday School teacher, Isaiah Birdsong,
chooses *sacrifice* as the topic of his lesson, Isabel wonders why—but
not for long. Isabel is obviously Isaiah's target when he declares one
sometimes must make a sacrifice "so that the people could live together happy and secure in their Christian lives." Then he addresses
Isabel, saying she surely knows the meaning of that kind of sacrifice.
Anger drives her to stand and deliver an impassioned confession in
which she tells the congregation what she believes is the story of her
father's death. Abruptly her confession becomes an accusation as she
narrates the cruel actions of her father: "For years you told us we had
to put up with it, . . . as if a man like my father was some terrible
affliction sent by God—a cross we had to bear." She continues, even
though both Mrs. Waters and the pastor attempt to squelch this angry
young woman:

> You may say, when I am finished, that I stood before you
> and confessed to fornication. Or maybe you think it
> doesn't matter whether I do or not, since everyone knows
> that I drove down into the breaks in a car alone with a
> man that is my friend. The appearance of evil to you is
> the same as evil itself, so I might as well plead guilty
> before you. Whatever you may think, though, I am not
> confessing. That sin is not mine to confess. All I want now
> is to ask you one question, and then I promise I'll be
> silent. Even if I had done all you seem to be accusing me
> of, why shouldn't you protect me, shield me, as you have
> done my brother, and for my sake—as well as his—refuse
> the truth? (267)

Archie, who has attended the service without telling Isabel he would be there, rescues her from the angry congregation.

Shortly, Isabel must face the real truth. Burnie, not Ray, shot their father from his hiding place in the barn loft. Ray's confession was meant to protect his sensitive, crippled, and bitter brother. When Archie brings Isabel home that Sunday, Burnie ambushes him with a rifle, inflicting a shoulder wound. Afterward, Burnie runs away from the family across the field to the railroad, where he is hit and killed by an oncoming train. When the Waters come to tell Lizzie her son is the victim of an accident, she says calmly, "We had better have the truth, Mr. Waters. . . . We have done without the truth too long, and it's done us no good. If Burnie was hit by a train, he's not hurt—he is dead. And if he was on the railroad track in front of the train, that was no accidint [*sic*]" (263). Lizzie Doane retreats into mindless passivity forever, and Greenfields is left to deal with the consequences of a morality that values appearance in human interaction and ignores the truth if it contradicts what citizens want to believe is true.

Joanna's storytelling granddaughter concludes this tragic story with an epilogue in which she records what happened to the main players in the Greenfields tragedy—but not before Rushing plays a subtle trick on the reader. The last chapter is an excerpt from Isabel's diary in which she records her romantic though painful evening with Archie after they witness the marriage of Joanna and Ray. She writes that finally Archie impulsively urges her to marry him that very evening. He knows the country clerk and can get a license. She concludes:

> The thing I'd never guessed at till I met Archie Hastings was better than I ever dreamed it would be. In his arms I did indeed forget everything—all anguish, all regret, all consciousness of evil. . . . I hope in that room down the hall Joanna was forgetting too. But she, it may be, had nothing that she needed to forget. (300)

With the quiet wit Rushing often demonstrates, she immediately rejects this all-too-typical formulaic story ending concocted in the purple prose of the romance. Isabel is only dreaming in her diary about what might have been. She confesses then:

> I have written all that because it is, in one way, true. It truly is what might have been. I remember when he called me Maud Muller that day in the garden, and I thought then that poem came too near the way things really had to be for us. And it seemed to me those lines were a prophecy: *Of all sad words of tongue or pen, / The saddest are these: it might have been.* (300)

What she and Archie have really decided that last evening together is that Isabel will accept Miss Lona's invitation to study for a year at East Texas Normal College. Archie's predictions for her future reveal perhaps his own uncertainty about this unusually bright young woman, who in the harsh language of class distinctions today might have been called "poor white trash." He assures her: "We'll write. A year won't be so long. And you'll read lots of books and learn all kinds of things. You won't be able to call yourself an ignorant country girl anymore" (301).

Looking back in the epilogue, the narrator reveals Isabel Doane never married. If indeed she never thought of herself as trash, her conversations before she left for school disclosed her secret worry that evil would continue to haunt the Doane family. Isabel's sense of doom seems fulfilled by Archie's death as a World War I flyer. From papers sent to her upon her grandmother Joanna's death, the narrator finally learns that Isabel became a sociologist, a professor, and an author. Her books and articles were considered pioneer studies of the role of women and children in the family. Significantly, among those papers is a box labeled "Unhappy Families," which contains many years of clip-

pings chronicling the deaths of men killed by their wives or their children. A cryptic note in Isabel's handwriting appears in the margin of
the story of a later Greenfields murder trial. The victim's wife and
daughter had hired a killer to perform the deed. They were convicted.
Isabel writes, "What would verdict have been if they had done the
killing?" (304)

Winds of Blame inspired two critical essays comparing Rushing's
themes to those of two other writers whose works appeared in the
early 1980s. Book critic Judyth Rigler prefaces her essay in *Texas
Books in Review* (1984) with the quotation Rushing has included on
her inscription page: Pope John Paul II's declaration that "[t]he truth
is not always the same as majority opinion." She judges *Winds of
Blame* a more traditional novel than Shelby Hearon's *Afternoon of a
Faun* and *Group Therapy*. Similarities between the two writers include
their examination of the conflict between illusion and reality as
theme and their sense of place, "as setting, as justification or catalyst
for behavior, as constant." Rigler's final assessment of Rushing's treatment of place echoes what Jane Rushing has said herself about her
persistent use of her native region as a setting. Rigler concludes,
"Rushing is content to describe the place she knows best, West Texas,
as she has in all her fiction. Her haunting evocations of that place
make the books ring true and clean" (23).

In an essay appearing in the *Journal of American Culture*, the scholar
Joyce Thompson examines *Winds of Blame* and Jane Roberts Woods's
The Train to Estelline as novels portraying West Texas farming community life in the early twentieth century. She too sees a similarity of
theme in both novels—the probing of dark secrets of community life
where the "inhabitants contrive not to know what they do not want
to know." Thompson adds, "In both novels the coming of age of the
protagonists rests on their discoveries of truths and their decisions
about what to do with their discoveries" (69). For Thompson, as for

Rigler, Rushing's story explores the power evil has for corrupting a people who chooses to ignore rather than confront its presence in their community.

Once again, in *Winds of Blame*, with its motivated, believable characters and realistic evocation of West Texas life, Rushing has demonstrated she is not simply theorizing when she declares that "[p]lace is made up of landscape, climate, manners and moral, culture and customs; and characters are largely made up their response to all of these" ("People and Place" 10).

In recognition of Jane Rushing's accomplishments, in 1984 *Winds of Blame* received the first annual $1,500 Texas Literary Award for fiction, an award sponsored jointly by the Southwestern Booksellers Association and the now-defunct *Dallas Times Herald*. Rushing's longtime editor at Doubleday, Sally Arteseros, sent a review copy of the novel to Pat Bennett with a note praising the novel as an "extraordinary work." *Winds of Blame* was Doubleday's last publication of Rushing's work as well as the author's final long work of fiction.

✦ Chapter 6 ✦

THE NOVELIST AND
OTHER GENRES

FOR MORE THAN A DOZEN YEARS, Rushing, a trained journalist and experienced researcher, remained resolutely determined to
capture in fiction the essence of the landscape and people she knew so
well. She seems to have written nonfiction on request from an editor,
including her essays on her process of writing, which appeared during
that time in *The Writer*. After she had published her first four novels,
however, an invitation to test her abilities as coauthor of an informal
history offered an opportunity to work in a different genre. Simultaneously, when Rushing began work on her novel, *The Raincrow*, she
also began collaboration with Kline A. Nall, a Texas Tech University
(then Texas Technological College) English professor, on a history of
the school. Time to work on her novel evaporated as she and Professor Nall tackled the arduous job of researching and writing *Evolution
of a University* early in the 1970s.

Impatient with the chore that writing the history became, Rushing prevailed to finish the project successfully, but she would not
attempt nonfiction again until near the end of her career, when she
returned to her roots to write *Starting from Pyron*, a combination
memoir and history of her home region. Her last successful work of
fiction appeared a year later in *Careless Weeds: Six Texas Novellas*, edited
by Tom Pilkington in 1993. Pilkington defines this genre, a form
Rushing attempted only once, by pointing out that the novella

demonstrates literary characteristics of both the short story and the full-length novel, requiring the sharp focus of a short story as well as the motivated change in the protagonist that one expects in a novel (xii–xiii). Although the history of Texas Tech was of limited interest to readers, Rushing's experiments in writing both her combination memoir and regional history and her novella produced readable and often illuminating examples of those genres.

Evolution of a University (1975)

Jane Rushing's loyalty to Texas Technological College, from which she earned three degrees, may have been the motivation for her decision to become involved in writing the school's history with her colleague, Kline Nall. In a letter to her friend, Pat Bennett, Rushing points out that the coauthors' purpose in writing the history was to try to say "something about Tech and its characters and its relation to the people of this area that we thought needed saying" (November 5, 1981). In 1975, the year Texas Tech celebrated its fiftieth anniversary, Rushing and Nall published their history despite difficulties in finding a publisher. Issued finally by Madrona Press in Austin, *Evolution of a University* particularly explores the less than harmonious relationship between the town and the college during its developmental years.

Both Rushing and Nall had become involved in the controversy developing around the proposed name change for the college in the early seventies. In her interview with Shay Bennett, Rushing is characteristically candid about her reasons for tackling the research necessary to produce the manuscript, which originated in the writers' misgivings over changing the university's name from Texas Technological College to Texas Tech University. Both authors desired a name change, but viewed the final choice as inappropriate for a university now emphasizing the liberal arts as well as the sciences and technological training. Rushing explains how this aptly titled book evolved into a personal crusade:

Kline and I were both very active in trying to persuade the right people that Tech needed a new name. In working with it, we got interested in the reason Tech was founded and what it was intended to be. We thought a lot of people just didn't understand the nature of the University and we thought it would be a good idea to write a history of Texas Tech. One thing I was especially interested in and the thing which became the theme of the book, was the relationship of the institution and the local people. I don't know whether this is unique or not since I don't have much experience with other state colleges; but around here, [members of] the Lubbock city power structure have always felt that they could really run Texas Tech. They feel that they got it here and they deserve to say how things ought to go. This is becoming less of a factor, but it was definitely a factor in the name change affair. (S. Bennett 51)

In his introduction to Rushing's last work, *Starting from Pyron*, Texas critic and writer A. C. Greene points out that "the only true elements of history" are the lives that "went on or stayed, or changed" in a place (3). Rushing and her coauthor approach tracing the story of Texas Tech with the same philosophy of the nature of history in mind. Anecdotes and profiles of colorful administrators and faculty members humanize what might have been a dull recitation of dates and reports of board meetings and political interference as the university developed into a university serving West Texas. Politicos from thirty-seven West Texas towns lobbied to have the college located in their town, but in late January 1923, Governor Pat Neff signed a bill designating Lubbock as the school's future home. By 1925 the school accepted its first students. In a discussion of student life on a campus where administrators and town watchdogs aimed to keep student life circumspect, the coauthors' accounts of West Texas collegians' pranks calculated to shock their elders reflect Rushing's subtle, and often unexpected, humorous observations on human levity.

To enliven their narrative, the authors describe such escapades as the "pink-pajama episode" in 1926. On a December morning, according to the first issue of *La Ventana*, the Texas Tech yearbook, the campus woke up to see "the loveliest, daintiest pair of feminine pajamas imaginable" waving from a flagpole in front of Cheri Casa, a boys' boardinghouse. Further description of the pink lingerie waving and flaunting its "yellow and lacy daintiness in the astonished faces of the town of Lubbock and the Texas Tech" prompts Rushing and Nall to comment: "It is a little hard to visualize the yellow daintiness of pink pajamas, but the meaning of the symbol on the flag pole at the boys' boardinghouse comes clear through the years. The spirit celebrated in a contemporary song as 'collegiate' had come to Lubbock" (57).

Several years later, when students committed some midnight requisitioning of bricks during the Give-a-Brick campaign for building the campus museum, they demonstrated that their "collegiality" had become even more creative. This time, in 1940, Dr. William C. Holden, who had been appointed curator of a then-nonexistent campus museum, had launched a campaign to acquire 320,000 bricks to use in building the museum. Donated bricks were valued at two and one-half cents each. The authors, again with a smile, note that "Tech students who have since become leading Lubbock citizens sometimes helped residents to donate without their knowledge; they like to joke now about where some of the bricks came from" (67). Recognizing the value of stories to enhance the readability of their history, the coauthors share campus lore they have heard or witnessed firsthand from the time Rushing arrived on campus in 1942.

By shelving other projects, the coauthors accomplished their goal of producing their university's history by the time the campus celebrated its fiftieth anniversary in 1975. Although the authors may have initiated the project with some thought of presenting the campus point of view in a "town versus gown" controversy, their attitudes toward city connections mellow as they chronicle the year-by-year growth of the college. Despite Rushing's condemnation of the anti-intellectual stance of the local newspaper and the often negative results of interference of city fathers in university affairs, by the 1940 campaign to build the museum, the tone of this joint effort to tell the story of Texas Tech begins to reflect the authors' loyalty and admiration for the school.

Texas Tech had by this time outgrown its reputation as a technical school and developed into a modern university with both a medical and a law school. The authors recognize as well that the town's support has continued to grow. To illustrate this positive connection with Lubbock's citizens, Rushing and Nall point out that "[a]s an illustration of cooperation between town and gown, the museum serves fantastically well." To begin the museum, the newly appointed museum curator found in the chemistry building attic "a son-of-a-gun stew pot with a hole in it, a pack saddle and an old branding iron." With generous contributions from Lubbock citizens, by the time the university celebrated its golden anniversary, the museum collection was housed in an imposing two-story building located on a seventy-six-acre campus tract that has become the Ranching Heritage Center.

Rushing may have regretted the time forfeited that she needed to finish *The Raincrow* manuscript, but in the end her experiment in both history writing and working in tandem with a colleague led to a satisfactory reward. She and Nall accomplished what they describe as their vision in the conclusion of their introduction:

> It has seemed to us that the history of Texas Tech University—because of the compression into such a comparatively short time of so much growth and change, and because of the intimate relationship of the college with

citizens of an area still close in time and character to the
Western frontier—serves uncommonly well to illustrate
the origins and development of the people's university of
America. (xiii)

Nine years after their history was published, Rushing was recognized for her success as a novelist and named a Distinguished Alumna
of both the Department of English at Texas Tech University in 1984
and of the College of Arts and Sciences in 1987. In 1988 the Department of Mass Communications honored Rushing as Outstanding
Alumna.

Starting from Pyron (1992)

Rushing completed *The Raincrow* soon after the university history
was published, and by 1983 the writer's work as a novelist ceased with
the publication of *Covenant of Grace* and *Winds of Blame*. For the next
few years, she exhibited little enthusiasm for writing fiction. She
wrote Pat Bennett that she just didn't want to write any more. Then
in 1987, she began to resuscitate the "Old Book," a project she had
thought would be her first book and her fervor for writing reignited.
She decided the Old Book was basically a good manuscript, full of
details of everyday life of Rolling Plains pioneer farmers including
the "Tom Sawyerish experiences" of her father and his friends as they
grew up in Pyron. By 1990 Texas Tech University Press requested her
revised manuscript and visualized a coffee-table book because it com-
bined both regional history and illustrative photos. She admits to
Bennett that she had dreamed about doing this book since she was a
twenty-one-year-old staff member of the *Abilene Reporter-News*.

Soon she revisited all of the places she wanted to include in her
revised history of Pyron. She writes to Bennett about some of her
thoughts as she returns to find places she remembers from her childhood no longer there and shares details of her goal for the book:

[O]f course my whole effort in this Pyron book is, in a
sense, to write about something that isn't there. I am trying to say that there is something still; but whatever it is
seems to exist largely in relation to the past. I have been
renewing my acquaintance with Pyron. It is gratifying to
me to discover that there are a lot of people still who
think they live at Pyron, even thought there is nothing
called Pyron anymore but a cemetery and a siding on the
railroad. Both of these are still in use, anyway. (October
14, 1990)

With her cousin Billie Roche Barnard as photographer, *Starting from Pyron* was published, as Rushing hoped, in time for the Pyron reunion in 1992.

It soon becomes obvious that what Rushing has called in her introduction to this book "the indelible stamp of *place* upon the human psyche" inspires her desire to recapture the landscape in which she thrived as a child. Appropriately, Rushing begins this combination memoir-history with her train trip as a five-year-old with her Grand-mother Adams. For this West Texas village that had hoped to be a flourishing town, the railroad became symbol of progress. It represents even more to the writer. In a later chapter, Rushing comments that "when the railroad first came to a dry little West Texas settlement, it was almost as though a mighty river had begun to flow through the land" (31). Rushing's father entertained his grandson with tales of his escapades involving hanging freights that came through the region, detonating dynamite he and his friends found abandoned by railroad construction crews, releasing the brakes on a sidetracked gondola car and taking a long ride through the breaks. Tom Sawyer could hardly have had more exciting adventures on the Mississippi.

For Pyron the railroad became "the shaping principle," Rushing says; but in the second chapter, she describes the Anglo settlers who came before the railroad. Bob Pyron settled on at least twelve sections

of the Breaks on a tributary of the Clear Fork of the Brazos in the late
1880s. Described as having "four daughters and a fiddle," Pyron
brought the ranch culture to the region, a culture that farm families,
who came a few years later, suspected did not honor their own fundamentalist Protestant moral code. For one thing, they disapproved of
Bob Pyron providing music for dances in his somewhat more elegant
home than the farmers built. The farm families disdained dancing as
recreation, but they nevertheless accepted Bob Pyron's generous gift
of land for a cemetery and his establishment of the first area school in
a dugout under his kitchen.

Rushing learned much of the history of the Pyron ranch, which
later thrived under several owners, in her research to write an article,
"Pyron Ranch," which appeared in 1971 in *First Cattlemen of the Lower
Plains of West Texas*. The story of this region reflects what Rushing has
called "the two faces of West Texas land." A major theme in Rushing's
fiction develops the sometimes uneasy relationship between farmer
and cattleman, both of whom moved without much thought of their
differences from the Breaks to prairie regularly during the early years
of settlement. Socially, however, their families rarely mingled.

In her conclusion to "Pyron Ranch," Rushing explains the impor-
tance, nevertheless, of the ranch country even today to those who
make their living on the nearby farms:

> Yet in some hardly definable way, the ranch even now
> belongs to Pyron. It lies northward making a boundary
> for the community—always to the people there it is the
> "Pyron Ranch," and they wonder about the condition of
> the ranch house and how much is left of the crude red
> picture-writing which once, in a different sort of world,
> marked the site of picnics and kodacking parties. I have
> heard that young people still sometimes wander down to
> Buffalo Creek, and find their way to Paint Rock, but they
> tread on forbidden ground. In a sense, the Pyron Ranch

belongs to the past; but as no people can ever completely
separate itself from its history, the ranch will probably
remain a part of the community as long as there is anyone
who says he comes from Pyron. (21)

As in her analysis of the farmer-cattleman dichotomy, Rushing
provides further understanding in *Starting from Pyron* of the place and
people that have served as sources for her fictional landscapes and
characters. She provides details of cotton farming on the Rolling
Plains, the art of trading as a tool for survival, the history of schools in
the region, and, most important, her own sincerely felt emotions
when she returns to landmarks that helped form her vivid sense of
place. Because the tone of this work is also that of a generous admirer
of Pyron culture, Rushing may have written *Starting from Pyron* to
assure her West Texas readers that even though she has written hon-
estly in her fiction about regional foibles, she still has high regard for
her native region and its inhabitants. She concludes her memoir with
a summary of the strengths of communities such as Pyron. Despite
their "touch of xenophobia" and their conservatism in their religious
and family life, Rushing points out that they are neighborly and
honor ties of kinship without question. Rushing never allows sentimentalism to color her fiction, and she does not do so in this work;
but if her declaration that she is a regionalist strikes critics as provincial, here the writer defends her decision to write what she knows. In
an afterword to this work, Daryl Jones provides a definitive assessment
of Rushing's regionalism. He says, "Considered as a whole, Jane
Gilmore Rushing's West Texas novels create a fictive world that owes
its very substance to the rich store of source materials and experiences
recollected in *Starting from Pyron*" (151).

"Wayfaring Strangers"

Winds of Blame, which appeared in 1983, was Rushing's last published
novel; but in her letters to Pat Bennett she spoke of working on a

mystery novel, planning another historical novel set in the sixth or seventh century, and circulating a play and a "Scandinavian novel." However, she did not publish fiction again for a decade. In 1989 the late Suzanne Comer, then editor at the Southern Methodist University Press, and novelist Clay Reynolds began searching for novella manuscripts for a collection by Texas writers. Reynolds contacted Rushing, who submitted "Wayfaring Strangers." Comer wrote her an approving note before her untimely death in 1990, but Rushing heard no more about the project for some time. A year later, she learned her novella would be published in a collection titled *Careless Weeds*.

"Wayfaring Strangers" is featured as the first work in *Careless Weeds*, a title Reynolds suggested. He explains in a brief note prefacing the volume that West Texas careless weeds, prolific and hard to control, "remind those who have worn a laborer's calluses that they are harbingers of hard work, little reward." He adds that novellas often require, like eliminating careless weeds, considerable labor without much recompense. Rushing does not mention remuneration for "Wayfaring Strangers," but this publication gave her an opportunity to publish fiction one final time.

In the introduction to the collection, editor Tom Pilkington compares the novella to both the short story and the novel. He describes the short story as leading to an "epiphany" that will influence the protagonist's future but does not speculate on what that future will be. On the other hand, the novel requires much more space for "its leisurely march through time and a dense thicket of detail to a more or less definitive conclusion." The novella resembles a long short story, the editor says, but is "lengthy enough to show the passage of time, to describe not just the illumination of an epiphany but actual change in the character's motivation and behavior" (xii–xiii). "Wayfaring Strangers" meets this criteria, although the editor points out that Rushing's novella is the longest story in the collection.

In "Wayfaring Strangers," the author again introduces a Grandmother of West Texas, this time in the person of Grandma Stephens.

May, adopted by her Grandma and Grandpa Stephens, tells the story some years later as she remembers it. The thirteen-year-old's almost daily companions are George Earl Tadlock, whose large family lives nearby, and Rosie Fargo, whose mother is ill and whose father is usually out of work. Most dwellers in Perdue Springs are feeling the effects in 1931 of the Great Depression.

Located on a spring-fed creek, the little town site is on the edge of the Rough Creek ranching country in the once secluded setting Rushing describes in *Mary Dove*. Rushing refers to this region in *Starting from Pyron* as Camp Springs, which she says "was always a little more of a town than Pyron and it lasted longer, even though it was missed by both railroads and highways" (97). She adds that Pyron farmers brought their corn for milling in Camp Springs, but once you drove into "the low hills and little creeks that supply the headwaters of the Clear Fork of the Brazos . . . it was nothing like Pyron at all" (98). As a small child, Rushing lived in Camp Springs for four years and in her memories, the town always seemed to her to be "a story-book village, half real and half dream." In "Wayfaring Strangers," the author recaptures those images in her creation of Perdue Springs. Isolated, even in the 1930s, the village is self-sufficient with the services of Grandpa Stephens's blacksmith shop, two stores, a post office, a cotton gin, a schoolhouse, and a tabernacle to serve as a church.

In the late summer of 1931, two dark and sinister-looking strangers drive into Perdue Springs in a Model T truck with their blue and yellow striped living quarters perched on the back. Suspicious natives begin to investigate. May thinks they look funny and, later, that they talk funny. George Earl observes that the dark-haired woman "don't look like a Christian." They must be Dagos, the natives' label for outsiders with the coloring of these two. Strangers who seem different are objects of suspicion in Perdue Springs, and the older woman and young man are "pretty dark-complected," as Grandpa Stephens observes. The narrator explains:

> "Dark complected" covered a wide range, but the way
> Grandpa said it suggested someone alien and apart. There
> had never been anyone very dark or different in our vil-
> lage; it would scarcely be an exaggeration to say we
> thought the whole civilized world looked like us, or
> ought to. We knew better, of course; but our folklore
> taught us that different meant sinister or comic. (7)

When the strangers park their unconventional house among the willows near the creek, they soon satisfy the town citizens' curiosity about their livelihood. A sign announcing RAVEN READS THE FUTURE is posted at their campsite. Learning that their name is Concolorcorvo and that Raven is the woman's stage name as a fortune-teller only increases Perdue Springs inhabitants' suspicion that no good can come from the strangers' invasion of their quiet little town. Mrs. Raven and her son John are obviously gypsies, although Grandpa has speculated earlier that they are "Eyetalian" or "Egyptian." The mother reads Tarot cards. Her son, a magician, can play the guitar expertly.

Whatever the strangers' talents, a few citizens, including the influential and pious Mr. Goodacre, think the two should move on. From the domino players down at his shop, Grandpa Stephens has heard some interesting stories about the newcomers. For one thing, the community's surreptitious monitoring of the pair's daily activities furnishes considerable subject matter for the village gossips. They know about Mrs. Raven's reaction when the Gibson twins chased her huge black cat. The twins report that she "waved a long stick at them and cursed them in witch-talk." Grandma Stephens comments that she didn't "reckon them Gibson boys would know witch-talk from monkey jabber," which amuses Grandpa. May adds, "I think he was pleased to find Grandma was at least a little bit sympathetic toward the Dago. It would have been just like her not to be: she liked for people to fit into well understood patterns" (19).

May joins the village spies when she begins to watch her good friend Rosie's activities. She senses Rosie's infatuation with the strangers' way of life. May and George Earl learn that Rosie, who is two years older, is dancing and singing as John Concolorcorvo strums his guitar. May certainly does not want her grandmother to discover Rosie loves dancing. She explains why:

> Everybody in or around Perdue Springs, except for some
> of the folks over in the Rough Creek country, considered
> dancing to be a sin. That was ranching territory, and gen-
> erally speaking, cowboys dance. Even so, the old people
> thought it prudent to pretend they didn't. So what they
> did every once in a while, was to give a musicale (pro-
> nounced musical). . . . We sat in chairs placed around
> the walls of the room and listened to a group of men
> playing tunes on fiddles, guitars, mandolins, and I think
> a banjo. (21)

May remembers, however, that the older folks usually left early, and then the dancing began. Once when the younger couples began dancing before Grandma Stephens leaves, she declares she will never go to that home again. She has no idea that Rosie, who lives with the Stephens during the school year, often attends dances at Rough Creek.

With Mrs. Raven among the worshipers at Sunday School one Sunday, Rosie provides the special music. Without accompaniment she sings "Wayfaring Stranger," which none of her audience has ever heard. She moves her audience with the plaintive old ballad:

> I am a poor wayfaring stranger
> Traveling through this world below.
> There is no toil, no sickness, nor danger
> In that fair land to which I go.

May describes the effect Rosie's voice has on her: "As I recall, it seemed timeless—a song of sorrow and of faintly glimmering hope, a song in a sad minor key, rising to a high, keening melody that in the end seemed to make of the hope our greatest sorrow" (27).

May, touched and disturbed, tries to puzzle through in quiet thought just what she has witnessed that morning. She believes Rosie "knew that her singing was like music poured forth from the throat of a bird." May admits, "I got an inkling then that art wasn't necessarily pine trees, and mountains painted in dark gloomy oils, and understood for the first time that line in one of my favorite poems about 'profuse strains of unpremeditated art'" (27). May is already vaguely aware that their grandiose plans to become schoolteachers and room-mates, which she and Rosie had daydreamed into their quiet lives, would never come to pass.

That afternoon after Rosie's triumphant performance, neighborly Grandma Stephens's compassion overrules her strong belief that one must be careful not to seem unconventional. She goes to see Mrs. Raven, although she makes clear she does not approve of the strangers' lifestyle. When the fortune-teller urges Grandma to just call her Raven, Grandma who knows she can't pronounce Concolor-corvo, decides to address her hostess as Miz Raven, adding "I have to know somebody pretty well to use their Christian name." With what she thinks is subtle questioning, she attempts to discover why this strange pair has come to Perdue Springs. Mrs. Raven's explanation only adds to the mystery. The Hermit sent them, she says, referring to directions received from her Tarot cards. Grandma comments, "I don't know nothing about no hermit. . . . But I'd be surprised to learn he ever heard of Perdue Springs" (32). She later admits, "I still wouldn't know a tay-ro . . . if I met one in the crossroads at high noon." Grandma remains skeptical, because she has never read about tarot cards in the Bible; but Mrs. Raven finally becomes the inquisitor in the conversation. "Do you come to read me my sins?" she asks. Then Grandma apologizes for the unfriendliness of those attending Sunday school that morning and their obvious refusal to welcome Mrs. Raven. What astonishes Grandma most profoundly during her visit is Mrs. Raven's request that Rosie sing "Wayfaring Strangers" for her son John as she had sung it that morning. At Rosie's request, John accompanies her on his guitar. When she finishes her solo, John praises Rosie's performance as almost professional.

Soon May has to admit Rosie's coolness means the end of their long friendship. Rosie is also questioning traditional beliefs. In a little chat with Grandma, Rosie hints that any evidence God has any plan for her future is missing. Rosie is questioning Grandma's accepted belief that God has a divine purpose for human lives. Grandma sets her straight when Rosie says God cannot know what we are going to do before we do it. Grandma explains the basis for her simple belief: "I think . . . that we just have to do the best we can. Our striving is a part of what will be." Then she adds, "What is to be will be because it already is. Past, present, and future is all the same to God. He don't even know what time it is" (35). Rosie tells May later she doesn't know what Grandma means, but she does know it scares her.

Much to the relief of Perdue Springs citizens, after a few weeks, the strangers pack up their belongings and their striped house and leave without informing the town of their plans. Before their departure, May and George Earl speculate why Rosie, who until now had made their excursions a threesome, spends her time hidden near the creek listening to John's wild music. Rosie mopes after they leave, but the good women of the town now have a more profound concern than Rosie's activities to occupy their busy minds and hands. Rosie's mother is slowly dying from pellagra, a skin disease, evidence that Mrs. Fargo's real problem is malnutrition. Rosie's father rarely has a job, and what food comes into the house Rosie's mother gives to her many children.

Another problem also arises. In this year of Depression and drought, plans to have a school Christmas program and tree seem doomed. Mr. Brock, the teacher, convinces his students that drawing

names for gift giving would make it difficult for parents battling hard
times. His students groan, "but not much. After all, we did know about
hard times" (51).

These community worries lead to an even more crucial common
concern. The strangers have returned. Cornelius Goodacre, justice of
peace and would-be keeper of Perdue Springs morals, begins a campaign to evict the "Dagos" from their camping place. He is indignant
when he discovers John Concolorcorvo shooting craps with the
town's young men. He knows, however, that Perdue Springs has
always harbored crapshooters, who are as much a part of the little
town as the domino players, and that his nephew is one of the regular
players. He is particularly incensed when John volunteers to provide a
magic show for their Christmas program. Also disapproving are
Grandma Stephens and a few other Perdue Springs women who live
by their treasured precept that one judged by appearance any departure from their notions of right living. Nevertheless, the magic show
wins most of the town citizens' enthusiastic approval.

Winter brings hardship; summer more drought. Grandma Stephens
recognizes that Mrs. Raven is not well. May knows Rosie has quit
doing her schoolwork. When Rosie responds to May's nagging in a
desperate effort to reconstruct their daydreams, Rosie says, "Oh, May,
grow up." Even more devastating for May is Rosie's contempt for
"that silly stuff about crows and statues and purple curtains." This is
her way of rejecting May's romantic description of the house they
would live in, modeled obviously on images from her reading. After a
shoving, slapping match, the two friends become enemies and never
speak again (59).

Grandma has befriended Mrs. Raven, but she is reluctant to
approve when the two Concolorcorvos decide to stage a show and
charge admission. Mrs. Raven is no longer well enough to tell for-
tunes. Encouraged by those who enjoyed the Christmas magic show,
the entertainers announce an even more spectacular show to be held
in the community tabernacle. Mr. Goodacre aims to put a stop to that

plan by reading the town's constitution and bylaws to John. Grandpa Stephens reminds the zealous justice of peace that no such laws exist. Goodacre capitulates, but he makes sure to have a seat on the front row to monitor the show. John's magic amazes his audience once again, but their astonishment becomes wonder when Rosie takes center stage, dressed in the sexy red dress John's dead wife had worn as the dancer Sheba. Rosie sings "Wayfaring Stranger" once again and then to John's guitar version of "La Golondrina," Rosie's dancing surprises and enthralls the crowd—all but Grandma Stephens, who walks out when Rosie drops her shawl to reveal she is wearing the low-cut costume Grandma has seen on a poster in the Concolorcorvo's truck during a visit with Mrs. Raven. Later, she learns Mrs. Raven has altered the dress for modesty's sake. Nevertheless, Mr. Goodacre has John jailed for contributing to the delinquency of a minor. Grandma, seeing her duty, takes the altered dress to prove to the sheriff that Mr. Goodacre's charge is a bit hysterical; but before John's release, his mother drops dead on her way to ask the Stephens for help.

Grandma defies Mr. Goodacre when he insists Mrs. Raven's body should not have been moved from the rocky path until a doctor declared her dead. Grandma tells Goodacre that if he thinks she will allow that "poor woman" to lie in the hot sun, he is crazier than he was when he had John thrown into jail, which, she adds, probably killed John's mother. Goodacre knows when he is outmatched. Not many days later, George Earl and May stand hand in hand as John Concolorcovo and Rosie drive out of Perdue Springs together, unaware of the two bereft friends watching them roll by, "laughing and talking. Rosie never turned her head" (88). Goodacre once again has to admit he has been outflanked. He has married Rosie and John the day before with Rosie's father as witness. "What else could I do?" he asks. Grandma Stephens, ever the believer in "what is to be will be," says, "There never was anything any of us could do, not from the very first" (81).

Rushing revealed in 1996, in a conversation with Ariel Peugh, that Grandma Stephens is her favorite Grandmother of West Texas (182). Strong in her religious convictions, sure of her moral standards, and generous with her granddaughter and her friends, who often look as though they need a good meal, Grandma Stephens illustrates Rushing's concept of the strengths that add dimension to the portrayal of this complex recurring character in her fiction. Grandma Stephens has common sense and compassion for the underdog. These qualities modify the rigid pattern that seems unchangeable in Rushing's characterization of Tamzen as a young woman in training to be a Grandmother of West Texas. What Tamzen will learn, as Granny Albright in *Against the Moon* and Grandma Stephens have, is that coping with the unpredictable in life will mellow the most inflexible personality.

Of her three ventures into writing other genres, "Wayfaring Strangers" most clearly demonstrates Rushing's continuing development as a competent and graceful writer. Her portrayal of characters with the complexity of Rosie's desires and the steady alteration of Grandma Stephens's opinion of Mrs. Raven creates a kind of tension her first novels failed to accomplish. Tom Pilkington notes that this work "moves at a slower pace than the other novellas," but, he adds, "Rushing's prose, as in all her fiction, is lucid and precise" (xiv).

Chapter 7

WEST TEXAS FROM A
WOMAN'S POINT OF VIEW

ANALYSIS OF RUSHING'S CANON leads to awareness of her
two major accomplishments as a regional writer. For the first time, a
West Texas novelist presents the life and history of the last Texas frontier from a woman's point of view. Except in *Walnut Grove*, her first
novel, Rushing's protagonists are women, who in their responses to
personal upheaval, family life, local history, and community activity
reveal their own strengths and weaknesses. To achieve the realism
characteristic of these narratives, Rushing also firmly establishes that
she has a thorough knowledge of the history of the Rolling Plains and
demonstrates that she is not afraid to be truthful about both the people and the place in her works.

Jane Gilmore's birth in 1925 occurred scarcely three decades after
the first ranchers and farmers settled in her native region. For the history of the area before she began to take note, Jane found her parents
and relatives, all accomplished storytellers, provided rich resources for
the human history of the Rolling Plains. A good listener from the
beginning of her writing career, Rushing also became a careful
observer of landscape and of people. An apt example of the writer's
skill in both capturing place and establishing symbolic significance
associated with landscape comes early in *The Raincrow* when Gail
Stoneman describes her thoughts as she awakens in her old room:

> Sunday morning the raincrow is back. I awake to scissor-
> tail snippings, and then as I lie in bed watching elm-leaf

shapes against the pale western sky, the raucous rain call
comes. Raucous may not be exactly the right word for it,
but it is not really a pleasant sound, and only the mystery
of its origin, established in my childhood, could account
for the old sense I had of its being a mystic summons. I
can understand why some people consider it a bad luck
sign. Apart from any effect it might have on the weather,
there is something about it very like the raven's croak—
the explanation, no doubt of its old name. (74)

Rushing exhibits her knowledge of the elements of nature and the
emotions those elements arouse in all of her fiction, and often that
knowledge emerges from how her women characters relate to nature
in West Texas.

To communicate her vision of West Texas life from a woman's
point of view and to do that without flinching when the truth must
be told, Rushing demonstrates several techniques for characterizing
complex and believable women characters. She creates at least three
types of women without resorting to stereotype. One of her reoccur-
ring portrayals is that of the already discussed Grandmother of West
Texas, who is usually rigid in her adherence to her religion-inspired
moral code, but as mother, wife, and neighbor, varies perceptibly in
each novel in which she appears. Two of these types, Mrs. Bailey in
Walnut Grove and Mrs. Waters in *Winds of Blame*, monitor the behavior of their daughters and friends, frequently warning that how their
actions appear to others will tell both friends and enemies how virtu-
ous they are. Rushing's most convincing tool for conveying the personalities of these women is her ability to capture tone in what they
say. When Joanna questions her mother, Mrs. Waters, about the
woman Isabel's father has brought home in *Winds of Blame*, she
detects anger and frustration in her mother's answer:

[T]his was a tone of voice Joanna was well acquainted

with: there was a challenge in it, as though whoever she
was speaking to was responsible for all the immorality in
the community. And there was fire in it, which burned in
her righteous indignation that such a scandal could take
place in Greenfields. It made Joanna feel accused,
denounced; and half believing that through her association with the Doanes she really bore the blame, she began
to cry and fled to her room. (88)

Earlier, Joanna's mother has voiced a warning about Ray Doane,
Joanna's fiancé: "You had better think a long time about whether
[Ray] might turn out just like his dad." Only occasionally does Rushing describe the physical appearance of these women, but how they
respond to family problems and community crisis clarifies their roles
as keepers of the community mores.

On the other hand, Gail Stoneman's mother, Laura Messenger,
represents the hard-working, understanding women Rushing introduces as John Carlile's mother in *Walnut Grove* and describes as the
dying Granny Albright in *Against the Moon*. Granny Albright knows
the youthful failings of her granddaughter Maurine, but offers only
comforting advice rather than harsh criticism. Another of these big-
hearted women, Laura Messenger, encourages Gail's son Paul to stay
in West Texas because he is a "born farmer" and persuades Gail her
son should be free to follow his dreams.

Grandma Stephens in "Wayfaring Strangers" illustrates Rushing's
understanding of the ambivalent spirits these women sometimes dis-
close in their actions. Grandma Stephens visits Mrs. Raven at her
campsite out of curiosity and suspicion; but in the end, her good heart
and neighborly concern influence her relationship with this woman,
different in nationality and in her domestic life. Again, more with dialogue and description of action than with detailed discussion of physical attributes, Rushing characterizes these women whose compassion
overrules their need to control. In a conciliatory mood when she vis-

its Mrs. Raven in "Wayfaring Strangers" and apologetic for Perdue
Springs' lack of hospitality, Grandma Stephens explains, "What it is, I
think,. . . is that we just ain't used to strangers." She continues, "Or just
anybody we don't understand. And there's a lot we don't, because we
live kind of cut off from the world, in a way" (49–50). Grandma's
struggle to understand outsiders will lead to the practical wisdom
Granny Albright has achieved in a lifetime of warmhearted response
to family and community crises.

Rushing discusses her understanding of this recurring character in
her work when she says the Grandmother figure passed along a mixed
heritage to her grandchildren. The author explains:

> If we who are her granddaughters find ourselves among
> the lucky ones, we inherit her strength and determina-
> tion, the will to work and the challenge of a job well
> done, the sense of responsibility for our loved ones and a
> healthy concern for the well-being of our communities.
> Too often the balance goes in favor of the looks of the
> thing, and we are left confused about the realities of our
> lives. When I have thought enough about this aspect of
> the Grandmother myth, I may at last be able to write
> effectively about the granddaughters. ("The Grand-
> mother" 44–45)

Rushing made this appraisal of the Grandmother myth in 1983,
but six years earlier in *The Raincrow*, she had already introduced one
of those granddaughters as the second type among her women characters. These younger women demonstrate ambivalence in their
efforts to dismiss attitudes they grew up with as daughters of the
Grandmothers. When she was a child, Gail remembers a visit by Laura
Messenger's friend Nadine, who was divorced and back in Walnut
Grove from California, a sinner in her parents' eyes, but glad to be
home for a while. Gail herself will later become a divorced professor

from California, back for the summer in her mother's home and just as unsure of her future as she remembers Nadine's uncertainty about her life.

Characterization of these women with variations in Rushing's fiction depends on her observation that intellectual or artistically gifted women, usually young and restless, must leave, as she did, the sometimes stultifying atmosphere of their homeland if they are to grow as persons. Sometimes they succeed; sometimes they remain restless, searching individuals. Rosie Fargo in "Wayfaring Strangers" wants only to express her emotions in dance and song, but to do so she must leave Perdue Springs with John Concolorcorvo, who has brought music into her poverty-stricken life. Isabel Doane in *Winds of Blame* finally recognizes that Greenfields offers no opportunity for growth mentally or emotionally and leaves for college, later to become a sociologist and researcher into family life. These women escape the Rolling Plains, but their departure does not always lead to fulfillment as Gail Stoneman has discovered.

One other three-dimensional female character, usually anxious to escape the grandmother's vigilance, often also possesses positive traits of the grandmother. These women assume a different role in Rushing's fiction because they mature, even as middle-aged women, and begin to see their own imperfections. By the conclusion of *The Raincrow*, Gail Stoneman seems to have finally recognized her own selfish preoccupation with her personal life. She reconciles completely with her mother. She accepts without question her son Paul's decision to follow his own dream. She promises him she will return to California and get to know her neighbors, the Zimmermans, symbolic apparently of her gradual realization that self-involvement does not lead to the peace she hoped to find in her return to Walnut Grove. Granny Albright's middle-aged granddaughter, Maurine, has never left home, and her life has not been what she hoped. During the days of Granny's dying, Maurine begins to understand family relationships and exemplifies maturity in her involvement in family conflicts. She becomes the connecting link between Granny's comforting wisdom in the times adversity mars life and the young bride Linda Kay's aimless search for her identity and the adolescent Debora's struggle to grow up.

Although this Grandmother myth influences the creation of many of the women in Rushing's work, she includes realistic depictions of other types: the downtrodden Lizzie Doane and the prostitute Alma Greeping in *Winds of Blame*; Gail Stoneman's cousin Hugh's wife, the materialistic but good-natured Tommye Jo in *The Raincrow*; the self-righteous Juanita and the innocent Linda Kay in *Against the Moon*; the charismatic Anne Hutchinson in *Covenant of Grace*; and the unlettered biracial Mary Dove. Point of view usually originates in the third person voice of a major woman character in most of Rushing's fiction, but there are exceptions. "Wayfaring Strangers" is narrated by May Stephens, as an adult remembering that summer of upheaval in Perdue Springs when she was thirteen. Gail Messenger Stoneman, one of Rushing's favorite characters, describes her visit home in first-person, present tense, which gives immediacy to the narrative. When she remembers the past, she does so predictably in past tense.

Rushing employs another method of presenting the story from the first person point of view. As an inveterate journal writer from her own childhood, she often develops her plots through the diaries of major characters. Isabel carefully reasons out her situation in her diary, deciding somehow to marry Archie, even as she admits her mother desperately needs her companionship at the time (*Winds of Blame* 235–36). In *Against the Moon*, the adolescent Debora shares in her journal her impressions of her father's pursuit of cousin Linda Kay, relives her regret for killing the butterfly, and tries to decide why she feels so upset over the physical changes she is experiencing (156–58). In this novel, too, after her death, Granny Albright narrates some of her past life for Maurine in a letter she has given her some time before with instructions to wait until her death to read it. The letter's last words share Granny's sturdy philosophy of life: "It don't seem like my dying could cause much trouble, and I don't think my living has caused more than most. I am satisfied with that it is the most I could have hoped for in life, and I am ready to go when my time comes. But not a bit sooner" (191).

Along with diary entries and letters revealing her characters' thoughts and history, Rushing connects her narratives with references to the remembered past of the region during the earlier days of the settlement, as well as to the history of the "town that tried to be," Walnut Grove. In "Wayfaring Strangers," Grandma Stephens tries to explain to Mrs. Raven why the town is suspicious of dark strangers. She tells Mrs. Raven about the schoolteacher who called the town the place time forgot, and she has heard that "they run some folks out of the country because they didn't like their looks." Mrs. Raven guesses they were "dark." Grandma responds: "I ain't so sure I know the straight of it. It had something to do with a old sheepherder named Perdue or something like that" ("Wayfaring Strangers" 50). The town has been named after him, she thinks, but his name might have been Pardue or Pardee. This isolated 1930s settlement obviously occupies the area around the springs where the early settler Pardue lived with his dark daughter Mary Dove before the turn of the twentieth century. In *The Raincrow* Gail Messenger remembers stories she has heard about Walnut Grove and its naming. The story of Walnut Grove is mentioned in passing on the first page of *Winds of Blame*. Rushing, generous in her explanations of her process of writing, never mentions this linking of her novels as a deliberate act, though remembered history contributes to creation of a connected chronicle of Rolling Plains history in her fiction.

In his afterword to *Starting from Pyron*, literary critic Daryl Jones summarizes Rushing's accomplishments with this linking of her novels through place:

All six of Jane Gilmore Rushing's West Texas novels take place in and around the mythical West Texas town of Wal-

nut Grove, a rural community located on the Rolling
Plains. . . . Unmistakably the fictional counterpart of
Pyron, Walnut Grove and its surrounding landscape—like
William Faulkner's Yoknapatawpha County or Thomas
Hardy's Wessex—provide the novels both a defining
locale and an abundant source of character and incident.
Spanning roughly a hundred years, the novels together
paint a broad panorama of the land and its history. Against
the backdrop emerge vivid portraits of the people who
shaped the land and who were in turn shaped by it. Inso-
far as their stories dramatize archetypal phases of human
experience projected against the larger cycles of history
and of nature, the novels assume individually and collec-
tively the scope and resonance of myth. (148)

Several other stylistic devices characterize Rushing's fiction.
Because she has a keen ear for the vernacular speech of these West
Texans and an uncommon understanding of human personality,
Rushing's work also exhibits uncommon knowledge of human psy-
chology and motivation in her portrayal of character. She writes of
her approach to speech patterns in "People and Place":

Since place helps shape characters and what they do, it is
a factor in the way they talk, too. But this does not mean
that dialogue has to be dialect. You can almost completely
abolish any need for peculiar spellings to indicate pro-
nunciation, or even for regionalisms that would not be
understood widely, if you listen for rhythms in people's
speech and notice vocabulary. (12)

When Laura Messenger tells stories from her past life to her
daughter Gail in *The Raincrow,* her speech rhythms and use of local
idiom reveal how closely Rushing has listened to West Texas conver-

sations all of her life. Laura speaks of her early life with Gail's father, who later is killed in a car accident:

> [W]hen cotton picking time come round again, and he had to work hard all day and was tired at night, he begun to stay home again. And then a lot of times Buck and Uncle Nezer would come by on a Saturday night, and they would play dominoes, or maybe all four of us would set down together and play Forty-two. Sometimes, after a month or two of flying at [courting] Nadine—as we used to say— Buck would bring her to our house and we would play games or maybe just make coffee and talk. (81)

When Mr. Godwin shifts from his usual speech to black dialect in his impassioned testimony in church in *Walnut Grove*, the narrator describes how the shift leads to young John Carlile's sudden illumination: "He did not know when the change came, but he knew, suddenly, with a shiver in his breast, that there had been a change." At the same time, except for John, the impact of the words Mr. Godwin chooses here seems lost on fellow church members. Rushing obviously intends that paradox. Sam Flowers has said it best: "They think as long as they don't say it, it's not true" (215). That haunting theme reappears in all of Rushing's novels. With this shift in vernacular expression, John's revelation becomes the reader's, and both begin to understand that Mr. Godwin is black.

Not only does capturing personality through her choice of language reflect Rushing's technique for developing realistic characters, but images based on the folklore and customs she absorbed growing up also define regional culture. In *Against the Moon*, relatives provide new pennies to cover Granny's closed eyes after her death, a common practice in rural life in early Texas. In *Walnut Grove*, Rushing describes candy pullings, school programs, Christmas celebrations, and farming practices. John Carlile remembers his grandmother was buried on a cold, windy, and dismal November day. He remembers, too, that Mrs. Godwin said, "There's always a spell of bad weather when an old person dies" (46). Weather cycles are crucial to the plot of *Against the Moon* with all of the action happening as the moon wanes. The meals Tamzen serves and her efforts to make a home in dusty West Texas mirrors the stories Rushing's Grandmother Freeman told her.

One of Rushing's most chilling descriptions of an early regional practice is her narration of the rabbit drive in *Winds of Blame*. Greenfields farmers plagued by jackrabbits choose a day to spread out across the prairie and drive the rabbits into a pen with noisemakers. There they dispose of the animals by beating them to death with clubs. A picnic climaxes the gory day. The brutality of the assault is offensive to modern sensibility, and it was so for Isabel Doane; but Rushing includes the scene to emphasize the cruelty of Harvey Doane, who insists on clubbing rather then shooting the animals (52–55).

Less dramatic is the author's description of the art of piecing and quilting Joanna's Lone Star quilt in *Winds of Blame*. "The quilt was the visible, tangible symbol of a serious, well-considered promise sealed with parental, and, yes community approval," the narrator explains (86). The difference between modern California culture and the old ways of Walnut Grove become obvious in *The Raincrow*, when Gail Messenger helps prepare green Kentucky Wonder beans with her mother early one morning. She remembers that her mother puts beans on early— "she belongs to the old school that cooks vegetables all morning in plenty of water with a good-sized hunk of pork." Her mother tells her that young Paul, Gail's son, "likes 'em that way . . . as long as he's got plenty of corn bread and butter." Gail has to admit privately that Paul probably likes long-cooked beans better than the vegetables she so carefully prepared with a few drops of water, cooking only until done (*The Raincrow* 16–17).

Emphasis in Rushing's novels rests on strong characterization rather than development of plot, and one of the strengths of her portrayals of people is her sense of the ironic in her character's lives. Tamzen will marry a cowboy, but only when he agrees to become a farmer. Anne Hutchinson willingly serves colonial Boston neighbors in every need, yet John Cotton and John Winthrop see her as a threat to their notion of community harmony. In the village of Walnut Grove, settlers go to Mr. Godwin, carefully unacknowledged as black, for advice on farming and religion; and even more ironically, they erect a sign forbidding blacks to stop in their newly designated town site. In *Winds of Blame*, Greenfields' citizens choose to call a murder an accident as a way of relieving their guilt over their failure to confront Harvey Doane's abuse of his family. Most of her fiction develops Rushing's perception of the ironic in the West Texas life she has witnessed.

This sense of the ironic adds dimension to both characters and plot in Rushing's work, but her realistic portrayal of West Texans rarely depends on explicit description of her characters' sexual lives. For example, although Harvey Doane in *Winds of Blame* brings a prostitute to live with his family, the many days when he does not emerge from the dugout where Alma Greeping sleeps suggest his physical hunger for her. When his youngest daughter Sophie tells Isabel their father has abused her sexually, she simply says she has also been down in the dugout with Harvey and perceives, shockingly to Isabel, that as long as Alma stays in that dugout, she need not fear that her father will resume his attacks. Stanfield's attempted rape of Gail in *The Raincrow*, understated though the scene is, conveys the horror the teenage Gail experiences from her cousin's actions as well as his words. C. L. Sonnichsen, in his commentary on Western fiction, "Sex on the Lone Prairie," condemns several writers' dependence on "raw sex" to sell their books, but praises Jane Rushing along with the Montana novelist Dorothy Johnson for including as much sex as necessary to be convincing but no more. He says that in *The Raincrow*, Rushing, "a superior writer, . . . traces the mistakes of the fathers through three generations without using explicit sex for its own sake" (*Hopa-*

long to Hud 172). Dependent on suggestion rather than graphic description, Rushing nevertheless manages to convey the drama of physical connection in all of her fiction.

Rushing's techniques for creating motivated believable characters and verisimilitude in both setting and story invention are consistently effective, although rarely experimental. Even though she is not perceived as an innovator in style, Rushing's themes are revolutionary in intent. She denied often that she was a feminist, but her insistence on chronicling the history of West Texas as a woman's story is counter to most fictional and historical narratives written by men. Her deliberate upending of the traditional Western novel plot to reverse the winners and the losers in the often told story of conflict between homesteaders and cattlemen not only gives a woman nester the lead in *Tamzen*, but creates a book-loving cowboy, who is willing to become a farmer.

The most courageous theme governing Rushing's West Texas novels is her honest examination of racism and prejudice in West Texas communities. Few Texas writers were yet brave enough in the 1970s to build a plot around a three-dimensional, biracial woman protagonist or to describe the sexual connection of an Anglo cowboy and a mulatto girl. Rushing also dared to challenge her native region's religious hypocrisy with her strong condemnation of church control over Rolling Plains lives. She declares over and over that judging others by the "looks-of-the-thing" morality causes only pain for victims of the self-righteous. Her criticism of the society Rushing knows so well examines overall the universal concerns of the nature of evil, the meaning of human freedom, and the plight of the intellectual who comes to feel like an outsider in his own land.

Chapter 8

THE WRITER'S LAST YEARS

Rushing's confidence in her abilities grew steadily in the 1970s as Doubleday continued to publish her fiction. Her relationship with her publisher was firm. Never feeling a need for an agent, Rushing worked directly with her editor, Sally Arteseros, who assumed Margaret Cousins's position after Cousins left Doubleday in 1970. She signed contracts with Doubleday giving the publisher option on her next book, but she rarely consented to a dated deadline. She told Elder she felt such a contract limited her freedom.

Critical response to her sixth novel, *Covenant of Grace,* in 1982 confirmed Rushing's growing reputation, but Rushing began to sense Doubleday did not seem much interested in the book after its publication. She told Pat Bennett, who had praised *Covenant of Grace* as a well-wrought psychological novel, that she is not surprised the publisher has hardly promoted her novel since she had recently read an interview with him in *Publisher's Weekly.* He had declared that writers are just like ball players, and you have to develop them just like baseball clubs develop ball players. With her usual dry wit, Rushing says she does not predict she will ever get developed. Rushing's negative impressions of Doubleday's promotion of this novel may have originated in the fact that the publisher delayed its release several times—once because two other novels on Anne Hutchinson's life were in the works. She was given no reason for the second delay. Nevertheless,

Covenant of Grace merited more critical acclaim than any other novel she had written.

Whatever misgivings the writer felt about her relationship with her longtime publisher, she surely felt appreciated with the publication of her last novel, *Winds of Blame*. Editor Sally Arteseros sent a review copy to Pat Bennett with a note praising the novel as an "extraordinary work." Judyth Rigler considered the novel a "traditional piece of fiction," but she classifies Rushing as a competent writer, who skillfully explores the "appearance versus reality question" (23–24). Daryl Jones would later call this novel the "most thematically complex" of all Rushing's West Texas novels (150).

Her next submission to Doubleday, probably the "Scandinavian novel" she had once mentioned to Pat Bennett, was apparently at first rejected, but Arteseros suggested Rushing hire an agent to circulate her manuscripts. In a letter to Pat Bennett, she says she sent a manuscript to an agent Arteseros recommends. She finally loses track of the manuscript completely (May 24, 1987). In one letter she says she is considering writing a mystery novel and adds she made a trip to a nearby town to interview the sheriff there. The sheriff was noncommittal because he and his family had just lost a lawsuit, so she visited with the justice of peace, a "double-knit pants type of lady." In a humorous aside, she adds she does not consider herself a "double-knit pants type of lady," but the justice of peace gave them a tour of the courthouse (June 20, 1985). Later she admits she is struggling with her detective novel and apparently soon abandoned this creative effort. No record shows any further national publishers' acceptance of manuscripts or any success in Rushing's hiring an agent, although she did make a half-hearted effort.

In 1987 her letters reveal her lack of desire to write. During this time she traveled to England with her son James, who was doing graduate research at the British Museum. She wrote that she thought it was time to back off and let some ideas percolate. What she had in mind at this time was resurrecting the "Old Book," which she identified as her father's story of his boyhood as he has told it. She begins to examine publishers for possible publication of this work (January 4, 1987). Meanwhile, she and Jay began work on a project, which involved folklore. Before she began writing *Starting from Pyron*, Texas Tech University Press cooperated with the Rushings in preparing for production a book on quilting; but when another similar work appeared, they dropped their support and urged her to finish her memoir-history of Pyron based on her father's stories.

By 1990 the Pyron book was in process. She wrote Pat Bennett that she was "so excited about this." This is a book she has dreamed of writing for most of her writing career (August 20, 1990). By April 1991, she finished the manuscript and learned Texas Tech University Press would also issue a reprint of *Walnut Grove*. By 1991 when both *Walnut Grove* and *Against the Moon* were published in soft cover reprints by university presses, Rushing had obtained all rights to her seven novels from Doubleday.

Although she remained isolated on the High Plains throughout her career and rarely had contact with the Texas literary establishment, writers who came to Texas Tech as speakers added dimension to Rushing's creative life. In the late 1960s, Rushing participated with Larry McMurtry in a creative writing symposium at Texas Tech University. Rushing read a paper on *Against the Moon*, which had just been published, and McMurtry discussed *Horseman, Pass By*, his first novel, which caused a stir among members of the Texas literary establishment in 1961. Rushing presented her paper first, discussing problems she faced in finding the right narrator for *Against the Moon*. McMurtry admitted in his talk that he did not know whose story he should be telling in *Horseman, Pass By* until he saw the 1963 production of the movie *Hud*, which switches from the book's emphasis on portrayal of the teenager Lonnie to the antics of Lonnie's dissolute uncle Hud. Such indecision over which character should focus the narrative rarely challenges either writer again, although Rushing spent some weeks experimenting with point of view for *The Raincrow*.

In 1996 Rushing told her interviewer, Ariel Peugh, of her pleasure at serving as host to Eudora Welty, when the respected Southern writer came to Texas Tech University campus for a conference several years earlier. At dinner Rushing and Welty talked privately about writing and, most likely, of a writer's sense of place, because both writers have expressed their high regard for place as the most important factor in their creation of characters in their fiction. Later Welty wrote Rushing her thanks for the enjoyable evening (Peugh 38). In an earlier interview with Elder, Rushing described how Welty's fiction had inspired and influenced her. She said she did not try to write like Welty, but she added, "I think I have been inspired to look for character interpretations and have a sharper eye for the inner actions of the characters and a new sense of places through reading her books" (Elder 125).

Her only other work of fiction, "Wayfaring Strangers" was published ten years after she had produced *Winds of Blame*, her last novel. She continued to write during that decade, but she also devoted those years to traveling, taking a brief sabbatical from writing, and researching family and regional history. With the publication of *Starting from Pyron*, this unreconstructed regionalist came full circle in her career as chronicler of West Texas social history. "Wayfaring Strangers" was the last work Rushing published. Four years later, Jane Gilmore Rushing fell victim to cancer and died at age seventy-one on July 4, 1997. She is buried not in the Pyron Cemetery but in Lubbock.

Chapter 9

A WEST TEXAS WRITER'S LEGACY

WHAT PLACE IN TEXAS LETTERS has Jane Gilmore Rushing earned? She rarely left West Texas to promote her books. Although she was a member of the Texas Institute of Letters, few in the critical establishment have read all of her novels, evident in comments that her books lack substance or vision, usually based on the critic's knowledge of one or two of her works. In 1983 she served on the Literature Panel of the Texas Commission on the Arts, but admitted she knew few Texas writers. She boldly declared she was a regionalist, which she defended with the argument that all writers who believe in sense of place as essential to good storytelling believe life has to happen somewhere, so why not set your fiction in the region you know best.

Nevertheless, in her prime years, Rushing was recognized not only as a major writer by Doubleday but internationally with translations of several of her novels. Her career was launched by a prize-winning short story. Her last novel was awarded the Texas Literary Award for Fiction. James Ward Lee includes *Against the Moon* in his *Classics of Texas Fiction* and lists *Walnut Grove* and *The Raincrow* in his "Annotated Bibliography of Other Classics of Texas Fiction." A comprehensive reading of her seven novels will clearly convince that Rushing's work steadily became more complex psychologically and more literary in both style and structure. She told Pat Bennett late in her career in an interview published in the *Dallas Morning News* under the headline "Jane Rushing: Mixing Religion, Writing" that "[i]t sounds so

pompous to talk about the truth, . . . but I would like to say something
that could be regarded as an element of truth" (February 14, 1982).
She accomplished that modest goal without question.

Sandra Scofield, a native West Texan who has won numerous acco-
lades for her own novels, recently in a few words established Rushing's place in Texas letters. In her review of the posthumous collection
of short stories by another Texas writer, Mary Ladd Gavell, Scofield
links Rushing with another of Texas's most distinguished women
writers. She says, "[Gavell's] stories represent an old literary tradition
when an unstrained humor, candor and modesty were esteemed
above irony and authorial self-consciousness, and small, honorable
lives were natural subjects; think of Katherine Anne Porter and Jane
Gilmore Rushing." Scofield's commentary on the cover of the recent
reprint of *Mary Dove* expands her praise of the author's work:

> Jane Gilmore Rushing's body of work is a national treas-
> ure. It reminds us that we are all alike in this: our lives are
> lived moment by moment, day by day, and however far
> we travel, we carry our family, our birthplace, and our
> humanity with us. For sure Texas kids should read her
> work in high school, when their heads are full of deter-
> mination not to be their parents. I especially love her por-
> trayal of women, and the relationships among genera-
> tions. There is sadness in the reminder of what seems lost,
> but also joy in remembering. Rushing is proof that narra-
> tive saves us: our innocence, our past, our connections; it
> is our way to return, a way she demonstrates in gentle,
> modest, and artful prose.

Faulkner gives us Yoknapatawpha County, Welty reimagines the South
as place, Larry McMurtry examines life in the Southwest. Like these
writers, Rushing reconstructs the social history of her own region in
her own lucid, straightforward prose; and with this fictive history, she,

too, has earned attention as a fearless social critic. Even though she is a writer of plain style who rarely needs metaphor to convey her ideas, she is also an innovator in choice of theme. Few writers have captured the everyday lives of Texans who settled the Rolling Plains of Texas with a perceptive understanding of what motivated and governed those lives. Contemporary Texas writers Benjamin Capps and Elmer Kelton have depicted cowboy personality and cattlemen's lives authentically. Rushing on the other hand has shown what life was like for those tenacious women who were willing to accept the isolation, the wind, and the dust that was inevitable in this region as part of what otherwise was a promising life for them and their families if they worked hard and lived right, according to the religious precepts they have clung to since frontier days. If read casually and selectively, Rushing's straightforward storytelling may deserve complaints that her novels rarely attempt the experimental, but her strength as a novelist lies in the truthfulness and compassion with which she writes of place and individual in the region she knows well and a people she obviously understands.

Rushing found neither modernist experimental structure nor postmodernist emphasis on the meaninglessness of life compatible with old-fashioned storytelling. And none can deny she is a talented storyteller. Without sentimentalism or even nostalgia, Rushing writes an apt conclusion for her version of her native region's history. In some ways, it is also an apt conclusion for this study. She has visited the only surviving landmark of the town that once was Pyron. She experiences the cemetery as "a place of serenity and hope." She continues:

> I am grateful that I can still go there, as I did on a day in late autumn, and feel peace as almost a tangible presence. It was late in the day when I came there: the bushes cast long shadows, and evening gray was settling over breaks land. As I came through the gate, a flock of small birds

flew out of the dark old arborvitae that hump higher than
any other plant life there and make the only mark against
the sky. Once the whirring of their wings was stilled,
silence came down all around.

I took it as a valued gift, that time I spent there—with
the silence and the sinking down of day, and the land to
the east spread out so far that it became at last the color
of the sky and blended with it, leading on and on like the
promise of infinity. (145)

SELECTED BIBLIOGRAPHY

Primary Sources by Jane Gilmore Rushing

NOVELS

Against the Moon. Garden City, NY: Doubleday, 1968. Reprinted with introduction by the author. Fort Worth: Texas Christian Univ. Press, 1991.

Covenant of Grace. Garden City, NY: Doubleday, 1982.

Mary Dove. Garden City, NY: Doubleday, 1974. Reprint, Lubbock: Texas Tech Univ. Press, 2003.

The Raincrow. Garden City, NY: Doubleday, 1977.

Tamzen. Garden City, NY: Doubleday, 1972.

Walnut Grove. Garden City, NY: Doubleday, 1964. Reprinted with introduction by the author. Lubbock: Texas Tech Univ. Press, 1992.

Winds of Blame. Garden City, NY: Doubleday, 1983.

FICTION IN PERIODICALS AND COLLECTIONS

"Against the Moon." *Virginia Quarterly Review* 37 (1961): 376–90.

"Against the Moon." In *Let's Hear It: Stories by Texas Women Writers*. Ed. Sylvia Ann Grider and Lou Halsell Rodenberger. College Station: Texas A&M Univ. Press, 2003. 203–13.

"Against the Moon." In *Her Work: Stories by Texas Women*. Ed. Lou Halsell Rodenberger. Bryan, TX: Shearer, 1982. 234–46.

"Albright Women." *Redbook* (May 1968): 155–77.

"Raincrow." *Redbook* (July 1977): 173–95.

"Walnut Grove." *Redbook* (December 1997): 197–219.

"Wayfaring Strangers." In *Careless Weeds: Six Texas Novellas*. Ed. Tom Pilkington. Dallas, TX: Southern Methodist Univ. Press, 1993. 3–81.

NONFICTION BOOKS

Evolution of a University: Texas Tech's First Fifty Years. With Kline A. Nall. Austin, TX: Madrona, 1975.

Starting from Pyron. Lubbock: Texas Tech Univ. Press, 1992.

UNCOLLECTED ARTICLES AND INTRODUCTIONS

"People and Place." *The Writer* (September 1969): 9–12.

"Pyron Ranch." In *First Cattlemen On the Lower Plains of West Texas*. Compiled by the Snyder Unit of the Ranch Headquarters Association, 1971. 20–21.

"Camp Springs." In *Early Ranching and Water Sources in West Texas*. Compiled by the Snyder Unit of the Ranch Headquarters Association, 1971. 35–37.

"The Roots of the Novel." *The Writer* (July 1975): 9–11, 46.

"Memories of Growing Up Off the Beaten Path." *Dallas Times Herald*, 25 July, 1982: 34.

"Setting in the Historical Novel." *The Writer* (September 1984): 13–15.

"The Grandmother of West Texas: The Myth of the Pioneer Woman in the Novels of Jane Gilmore Rushing." In *Texas Women: The Myth, the Reality*. Ed. Joyce Thompson. Denton: Texas Woman's Univ. Press, 1985. 39–45.

COLLECTIONS AND UNPUBLISHED MANUSCRIPTS

"Great-Grandmother's Letters: From the Correspondence of Margaret Elizabeth Gilmore." With Billie Roche Barnard. Lubbock, 1993.

"House Symbolism in the Work of Five New England Romanticists." PhD diss., Texas Technological College, 1957.

"Recollections of a West Texas Boyhood, 1897–1913." Lubbock, 1994.

Rushing Papers. Southwest Collection. Texas Tech Univ., Lubbock. Box A333.1A. Clippings, notes, and manuscript on history of Block 97, written for publication of Snyder branch of Ranch Headquarters Association. Manuscript of "Plans for a Novel about 'Block 97.'" Rough draft of *Tamzen*.

Selected Secondary Works

Bader, Barbara. Review of *Against the Moon,* by Jane Gilmore Rushing. *Kirkus Review* 15 April 1968: 483.

Bennett, Charlene W. [Shay]. "The Influence of Libraries in the Work of Four Texas Writers." Master's thesis, Texas Woman's Univ. December 1980.

Bennett, Patrick. "Jane Rushing: Mixing Religion, Writing." *Dallas Morning News* 14 February 1982: 5G.

Clark, Susan. "Hutchinson, a 17th Century Feminist." Review of *Covenant of Grace,* by Jane Gilmore Rushing. *Texas Observer* 6 August 1982: 20.

Davis, Kenneth W. "Pistols on the Wall: Traditional Narrative Elements in Modern Texas Fiction." *Concho River Review* 2, no. 1 (Spring 1988): 37–45.

Dillon, Gay Andrews. "Best of the Current Novels." Review of *Covenant of Grace,* by Jane Gilmore Rushing. *Christian Science Monitor* 21 July 1982.

Dobie, J. Frank. "A Preface with Some Revised Ideas." *Guide to Life and Literature of the Southwest*. Dallas: Southern Methodist Univ. Press, 1942: 1–8.

Elder, Iva Nell. *Gentle Giants: Women Writers in Texas.* Austin: Eakin Press, 1983: 118–26.

Eubank, Judith. "Healer or Heretic? The Story of Anne Hutchinson." Review of *Covenant of Grace,* by Jane Gilmore Rushing. *Dallas Morning News* 6 June 1982: 4G.

Green, A. C. Introduction to *Starting from Pyron.* Lubbock: Texas Tech Univ. Press, 1992: 1–3.

Grider, Sylvia Ann, and Lou Halsell Rodenberger, eds. "Jane Gilmore Rushing." *Let's Hear It: Stories by Texas Women Writers.* College Station: Texas A&M University Press, 2003: 197–203.

Hill, William B. Review of *Mary Dove,* by Jane Gilmore Rushing. *America* 4 (May 1974): 348.

Jones, Daryl. "Jane Gilmore Rushing." In *Twentieth Century Writers.* Ed. James Vinson. Detroit: Gale, 1982: 675.

———. Afterword to *Starting from Pyron.* Lubbock: Texas Tech Univ. Press, 1993: 147–53.

Key, Cheryl. "Jane Gilmore Rushing: Social Historian of West Texas." Master's thesis, Angelo State Univ., 1986.

———, and Peggy Skaggs. "Jane Gilmore Rushing." In *Texas Women Writers: A Tradition of Their Own.* Ed. Sylvia Ann Grider and Lou Halsell Rodenberger. College Station: Texas A&M Univ. Press, 1997: 160–65.

Lee, James Ward. *Classics of Texas Fiction.* Dallas: E-Heart Press, 1987: 128–29, 174.

Levin, Martin. Review of *Mary Dove,* by Jane Gilmore Rushing. *New York Times Book Review* 17 March 1974: 38.

Lindstrom, Naomi. "The Novel in Texas: How Big a Patrimony?" *Texas Quarterly* 21, no. 2 (Summer 1976): 73–83.

Lynn, Sandra. "Texas, Women, Fiction." *Pawn Review* 4, no. 1 (1980–81): 2–17.

Matthews, Becky. "Gypwater and Lacy Mesquite: Gendered Views of West Texas." *Southwestern American Literature* 27, no. 2 (Spring 2002): 55–60.

———. "Writing the Un-Western: Jane Gilmore Rushing and *Mary Dove.*" *Concho River Review* 14, no. 2 (Fall 2000): 65–73.

Peugh, Ariel Durham. "Place in the Novels of Jane Gilmore Rushing." PhD diss., Texas Christian Univ., 1997.

Rigler, Judyth. "Appearance and Reality." Review of *Winds of Blame,* by Jane Gilmore Rushing. *Texas Books in Review* 6 (1984): 22–24.

Richardson, Hazel. "West Texas Sets Stage for Rushing's Fiction." *The Bryan Eagle* 25 September 1977.

Rodenberger, Lou Halsell. Afterword to *Against the Moon.* Fort Worth: Texas Christian Univ. Press, 1991: 213–19.

———. "The Creative Woman in the Works of Southwestern Women." *Southwestern American Literature* 13, no. 3 (Spring 1987): 13–30.

———. "Eve Calloway and Tamzen Greer: The Grandmothers of West Texas." *Southwestern American Literature* 27, no. 2 (Spring 2002): 37–45.

————. Introduction to *Mary Dove*. Lubbock: Texas Tech Univ. Press, 2003: v–x.

————. *Jane Gilmore Rushing*. Boise, ID: Boise State Univ. Western Writers Series, no. 118, 1995.

————. "Presidential Address: Texas Women Writers and Their 'Usable Past.'" *West Texas Historical Association Year Book* 62 (1996): 201–28.

————. "Texas Women Writers and Their Work: No Longer 'Lady Business.'" *Texas Libraries* 45 (Fall 1984): 124–28.

————. "Women As Literary Participants in Contemporary Events." *Women and Texas History: Selected Essays*. Ed. Fane Downs and Nancy Baker Jones. Austin: Texas State Historical Association, 1993: 158–67.

Scofield, Sandra. "Snapshots From A Quieter Era." *Dallas Morning News* 26 May 2002.

Scarborough, Dorothy. *The Wind*. Reprint of 1925 ed. (Harper's). Austin: Univ. of Texas Press, 1979.

Sonnichsen, C. L. "Sex on the Lone Prairee." [*sic*] *From Hopalong to Hud: Thoughts on Western Fiction*. College Station: Texas A&M Univ. Press, 1972: 157–175.

Thompson, Joyce. "Seeing Through the Veil: Concepts of Truth in Two West Texas Novels." *Journal of American Culture* 14 (Summer 1991): 69–74.

Tuska, Jon, and Vicki Piedarski, eds. "Jane Gilmore Rushing." *Encyclopedia of Frontier and Western Fiction*. New York: Hill Book, 1983: 299–300.

INDEX